M000239468

No-Hype
Options
Trading

Founded in 1807, John Wiley & Sons is the oldest independent publishing company in the United States. With offices in North America, Europe, Australia and Asia, Wiley is globally committed to developing and marketing print and electronic products and services for our customers' professional and personal knowledge and understanding.

The Wiley Trading series features books by traders who have survived the market's ever changing temperament and have prospered—some by reinventing systems, others by getting back to basics. Whether a novice trader, professional or somewhere in-between, these books will provide the advice and strategies needed to prosper today and well into the future.

For a list of available titles, please visit our Web site at www.Wiley Finance.com.

No-Hype Options Trading

Myths, Realities, and Strategies that Really Work

KERRY W. GIVEN, PhD (DR. DUKE)
*Founder and Managing Director,
Parkwood Capital, LLC*

WILEY

John Wiley & Sons, Inc.

Copyright © 2011 by Kerry W. Given. All rights reserved.

Published by John Wiley & Sons, Inc., Hoboken, New Jersey.
Published simultaneously in Canada.

No part of this publication may be reproduced, stored in a retrieval system, or transmitted in any form or by any means, electronic, mechanical, photocopying, recording, scanning, or otherwise, except as permitted under Section 107 or 108 of the 1976 United States Copyright Act, without either the prior written permission of the Publisher, or authorization through payment of the appropriate per-copy fee to the Copyright Clearance Center, Inc., 222 Rosewood Drive, Danvers, MA 01923, (978) 750-8400, fax (978) 646-8600, or on the Web at www.copyright.com. Requests to the Publisher for permission should be addressed to the Permissions Department, John Wiley & Sons, Inc., 111 River Street, Hoboken, NJ 07030, (201) 748-6011, fax (201) 748-6008, or online at http://www.wiley.com/go/permissions.

Limit of Liability/Disclaimer of Warranty: While the publisher and author have used their best efforts in preparing this book, they make no representations or warranties with respect to the accuracy or completeness of the contents of this book and specifically disclaim any implied warranties of merchantability or fitness for a particular purpose. No warranty may be created or extended by sales representatives or written sales materials. The advice and strategies contained herein may not be suitable for your situation. You should consult with a professional where appropriate. Neither the publisher nor author shall be liable for any loss of profit or any other commercial damages, including but not limited to special, incidental, consequential, or other damages.

For general information on our other products and services or for technical support, please contact our Customer Care Department within the United States at (800) 762-2974, outside the United States at (317) 572-3993 or fax (317) 572-4002.

Wiley also publishes its books in a variety of electronic formats. Some content that appears in print may not be available in electronic books. For more information about Wiley products, visit our web site at www.wiley.com.

ISBN 978-0-470-92015-2 (cloth); 978-0-470-94730-2 (ebk); 978-0-470-94731-9 (ebk); 978-0-470-94732-6 (ebk)

Printed in the United States of America

10 9 8 7 6 5 4 3 2 1

To Charlotte, my best friend, confidante, and adviser.

In memory of our son and fellow option trader, Sean (1975–2007).
I miss our discussions of Google.

Contents

Acknowledgments

S omeone wise once said that no man is an island. We are all the sum of not only our own efforts, but the love and contributions of many others. Of all of those who have influenced my life, my wife, Charlotte, stands out by far. I am a better person because of her being in my life.

I owe thanks to many teachers in my continuing journey of options education. The foundation of my options education came from Jim Bittman, Marty Kearney, and Russell Rhoads at the Options Institute of the Chicago Board Options Exchange. Several of my "aha" moments came through conversations with Jim Bittman in hallways and over lunches. Jim was very open about the "real-world" aspects of options trading often overlooked in the options education literature. I also owe a great debt to Dan Sheridan and Casey Platt for the personal coaching that honed my options trading skills. And I thank my editor, Kevin Commins, for his excellent advice and support.

Introduction

D oes the world need another options trading book? Before writing this book, I looked at all of the options books available on Amazon and it was daunting. But this book brings a different perspective to options trading. The existing options trading books fall broadly into two categories: (1) how to become financially independent in two weeks, and (2) how I made a fortune trading on the exchange floor. In the first case, it is largely marketing hype, and the second case describes trading options from a perspective that isn't realistic for the retail options trader. I admit this generalization does a disservice to several excellent options trading books, but exceptions do not invalidate generalizations.

My experience learning to trade options was lengthy and often painful. Trial and error characterized much of my learning curve. I spent large amounts of time and energy debunking many of the options trading myths. For those of you new to options trading, we will debunk those myths in the first few chapters of this book. But if you have some familiarity with options trading, you have probably heard or read the adage, *When implied volatility is high, sell credit spreads, and when implied volatility is low, buy debit spreads.* This is a classic example of a commonly taught rule for options trading that is absolutely false. The truth is that the credit spread and the debit spread at the same strike prices will always have the same risk/reward characteristics. Another instructor confidently assured me that out-of-the-money debit spreads would be successful 80% of the time and were "low risk." The truth is that those types of spreads have a very low probability of success—more like 25% than 80%. His options education firm likes to advertise those trades as low-risk trades because they require only a small investment. Lottery tickets are inexpensive as well.

Unfortunately, options education is infamous for outrageous marketing claims and sales pitches; for example, the following was a header on a web site for options education: "When was the last time you made 300% in three weeks?" In the overhyped world of trading education, it is exceedingly difficult to discern reasonable expectations for your returns with various trading strategies. This book will give you the foundation to develop a trading system with a probabilistic edge.

The end result of my "wandering in the wilderness" was the development of successful options trading systems for steady income generation. My objective with this book is to save you much of the time, effort, and losses that characterized my options trading learning process.

This book is unique in several key aspects:

- The author is a retail trader, just like you. This book describes trading strategies I use every day as a retail trader, not trading techniques that worked in the options trading pits several years ago.
- This book will give you the foundational knowledge of probabilities and options pricing that you need to survive and prosper in the options markets—nothing more and nothing less.
- This book will not clutter your mind with useless information like synthetics. Many instructors will teach you how to build combinations of stock and options to create positions that mimic other positions, thus the so-called *synthetic* position. For example, one may create a synthetic stock position by buying a call option and selling a put option to create a synthetic long stock position (i.e., this option position behaves exactly like owning the stock). Recognizing those relationships is crucial to the market maker on the floor, so he can hedge that position perfectly by shorting stock. However, synthetics aren't relevant for the retail options trader who is focused on conservative income generation.
- In this book, you have entered the No-Hype Zone. Many options trading education firms advertise examples of several hundred percent gains and claim to have discovered the "Holy Grail" of trading. Those are deceptive claims that have lured many unsuspecting traders into large losses in the markets. We will debunk the options trading myths and give you the basic knowledge necessary to turn your options trading into a profitable business.

Much of the options trading literature has been written by former options market makers and floor traders; many of the options trading instructors come from the same background. But the skills and knowledge necessary to be successful as market makers in the exchanges have little in common with the skills needed to succeed as a retail options trader. In fact, many of the personal characteristics that helped them succeed in those roles may be detrimental to the retail trader. The market maker must take every trade, and he must act quickly; volume is important in that business. But the retail trader can analyze trade candidates and market conditions and patiently wait for the optimal trade setup. Due to the speed and pace on the floor, market makers tend to be hyperactive personalities; calmly allowing a trade to develop over time would be against their nature. Retail traders can be very patient and deliberate and may trade only a few times per month.

So this options trading book is different. This book is focused on you, the retail trader, and it will give you the knowledge and the strategies to build an options trading business that generates steady monthly income. So let's get started!

No-Hype Options Trading

PART 1

The Foundations of Options Trading

CHAPTER 1

Option Basics

S tock options are members of a large group of varied financial instruments known as *derivatives;* that is, options are derived or based on shares of common stock or stock indexes. Unlike stock certificates, where there is a fixed number at any given point in time, option contracts are actually created as they are needed in the marketplace. One of the figures you will see in the option price chain on your broker's web site is "open interest," the number of contracts for that particular option that are outstanding at that point in time.

DEFINITIONS OF CALLS AND PUTS

A *call option* is effectively a contract giving the owner of the option the right to purchase a fixed quantity of stock within a particular period of time and at a specified price, the strike price. An example would be a December $200 call option for Apple Computer. The owner of this option has the right to buy 100 shares of Apple Computer stock for $200 per share anytime up until the December expiration, the Saturday following the third Friday in December.

A *put option* gives its owner the right to sell a fixed quantity of stock within a particular period of time and at a specified price. Analogous to the call option example, the December $200 put option for Apple Computer gives the owner of this option the right to sell 100 shares of Apple Computer stock for $200 per share anytime up until December expiration.

3

ARE YOU LONG OR SHORT?

In both stock and options trading, we refer to being *long* when we have purchased a security, as in: "I am long 200 shares of Apple Computer (AAPL)" or "I am long 10 contracts of the April $200 calls for AAPL."

Short refers to a security I have sold, so I can be short shares of AAPL stock or be short AAPL calls or puts that I have sold. When I am short stock, I have an obligation to buy the security at some future date to close the trade. The same is true when you are short options. However, with options, you may not have to close the position if the option expires worthless, but you would be wise to always remain aware of your obligations when you are short options. Many traders make it their practice to always buy back, or close, a short option position before expiration, even when it appears likely the options will expire worthless.

When we own options, we are said to be long those options, and if I have sold the options, I am said to be short those options. When I am short options, I no longer have a right to buy or sell stock as I did when I owned the options. The person who sold the call option has the obligation to sell the fixed quantity of stock at the specified price anytime before the option expires. If I sold the December $200 call for AAPL, I have an obligation to sell 100 shares of Apple Computer if that call option is exercised against me. The option's exercise is similar to the person to whom I sold the option coming to me and saying, "Sell me 100 shares of Apple Computer for $200 per share," and I don't have a choice; I have an obligation when I am short options. In a similar way, if I sold the December $200 put option for AAPL, I am obligated to purchase 100 shares of Apple Computer at $200 per share if the put option is exercised. When I am long an option, I always have the right to exercise that option and either buy or sell the underlying stock, but it is entirely my choice. When I am short options, I am obligated to buy or sell the underlying stock if the option is exercised. I don't have a choice.

OPTION CONTRACT SIZE

Options are bought and sold as contracts that normally cover 100-share lots of stock. There are exceptions, usually created by mergers and acquisitions where two stocks were combined, and an option may cover some other number of shares of the underlying stock. When you are perusing an options chain and see an option that appears to be more expensive than you would expect, based on the other options in that chain, that option may cover 125 shares (or some other number) rather than the standard 100 shares.

The option contract is priced on a per-share basis. For example, that Apple Computer $200 call may be offered for sale at $4.25. Since this contract covers 100 shares, we would pay $425 for one contract of the Apple $200 calls. The options contract is priced per share of the underlying stock to make it easier to see the relationship to the stock price.

IS MY OPTION IN- OR OUT-OF-THE-MONEY?

Options have a unique terminology that reflects the relationship of the option strike price to the current price of the underlying stock. If the strike price is close to the current stock price, we refer to that option (put or call) as *at-the-money* or ATM. Often, a stock price will be between strike prices, and the options on either side of the stock price will be considered ATM.

If the price of Apple Computer stock is $210, then I could exercise my $200 call option and buy 100 shares of Apple Computer for $200 per share or $20,000. I could then sell that stock in the market for $210 and have a gross profit of $1,000 (my net profit would depend on what I paid for the option). When the option has a net positive value if exercised, the option is said to be *in-the-money* or ITM. Call options with strike prices below the current stock price are ITM while put option prices with strike prices above the stock price are ITM.

However, if I owned the AAPL $200 call option and the current AAPL stock price had dropped to $198, I would not exercise the option; it wouldn't make sense to buy 100 shares of AAPL at $200 when I could buy those shares for less money in the open marketplace. These options are called *out-of-the-money* or OTM. Call options with strike prices above the current stock price are OTM while put option prices with strike prices below the stock price are OTM.

OPTION TRADE ORDERS

Since option contracts are created on demand in the marketplace, the orders for buying and selling options are more complex than the corresponding stock orders. If a trader wishes to buy an option, she has two choices. She may enter an order with her broker, usually via a web site, to *buy to open* or *buy to close*. These are often abbreviated BTO and BTC. I enter a BTO order when I do not have a position in that option and so I am

TABLE 1.1 Option Trade Order Terminology

Option Order	Shorthand	Action	Result
Buy to open	BTO	Buys a call or a put	Creates a long position
Sell to close	STC	Sells a call or a put	Closes the long position
Sell to open	STO	Sells a call or a put	Creates a short position
Buy to close	BTC	Buys a call or a put	Closes the short position

"opening" that position. At some later date, I might want to sell those options, and I would enter a *sell to close* or STC order.

We discussed short positions earlier in this section. If I sell an option when I do not already own that option, I am entering a *sell to open* or STO order and I will be short those options once this order is filled. When I wish to close that short position, I will enter a BTC order. Table 1.1 summaries the order terminology used for trading options.

OPTION EXPIRATION

Equity options expire on the Saturday following the third Friday of each month. It is common to hear or read that equity options expire on that third Friday because stock options cannot be traded after the close of the markets Friday afternoon. Saturday expiration allows the brokers to perform all of the exercises, purchases, and sales of stock on Saturday before the option contracts expire at midnight. Thus, traders often refer to "expiration Friday" and speak of the options expiring on Friday because this technicality of Saturday expiration has no relevance for traders.

However, some (but not all) index options cease trading at the close on the Thursday prior to expiration and those positions are reconciled on Saturday based on the settlement price established Friday morning. For example, the Standard & Poor's Index (SPX) options cannot be traded after the close on the Thursday before expiration, but the settlement price is established Friday morning based on the opening price of each of the 500 stocks that make up the SPX (the S&P 500). Since many stocks do not open immediately at the opening bell, the settlement price will differ from the SPX opening price Friday morning. The specifications for settlement and other characteristics of index options can be found on the web site of the exchange that creates the option. For example, the specifications of the SPX options are published on the Chicago Board Options Exchange web site, www.cboe.com.

LEAPS OPTIONS

A longer-term option was developed by the Chicago Board Options Exchange in 1990. These options are called Long-Term Equity Anticipation Securities (LEAPS). Not all stocks have options, and not all stocks with options have LEAPS. LEAPS have January expirations, and there are always two January options expirations available. For example, in June 2010, Apple Computer (AAPL) had two LEAPS options available, one expiring in January 2011, and another expiring in January 2012.

In general, LEAPS are used as surrogates for the stock itself. If one believes a stock is likely to appreciate greatly over the next year, he may buy the stock. But another trader with the same outlook for that stock could buy the LEAPS call option for a fraction of the capital required to buy the stock. There are two principal disadvantages of holding the LEAPS option instead of the stock; one is the loss of the dividends that are paid to the stockholder, and the other is the loss of value in the LEAPS option due to the passage of time. We will discuss this concept of "time decay" in Chapter 3 in more detail; for now, just realize that the price of the LEAPS option will slowly decline over time if the stock price simply trades sideways.

LEAPS are often substituted for the stock in classic stock/option strategies, such as the covered call (discussed in Chapter 5), or used to speculate on a longer-term bullish or bearish trend of a stock.

OPTION SETTLEMENT

Stock options are settled at expiration with shares of stock either being sold or purchased. If I hold a short position of three contracts of the $520 put options for Google and GOOG closes at $512 on the Friday of expiration week, then my option position will be exercised and 300 shares of GOOG will be purchased for my account at $520/share; that is, the stock was "put to me." Similarly, if I had owned five contracts of the $500 call options and GOOG closed at $512, I would own 500 shares of GOOG after the calls were exercised on my behalf. If I had been short the five contracts of the $500 call options and GOOG closed at $512, this would result in a short stock position of 500 shares of GOOG.

If I am long a call or put option, I may choose to exercise that option at any time before expiration. However, if my option is ITM by $0.01 or more, and I do not close the position before the close of trading on expiration Friday, my broker will automatically exercise that option on my behalf on that Saturday of expiration.

By contrast, index options settle in cash. If I own five contracts of the SPX $1,100 calls and the settlement price of SPX is determined to be $1,142 on expiration Friday, then my account will be credited with $21,000 (5 × (1142 − 1,100) × 100). But remember the unique settlement characteristics of many broad-based index options like SPX. They cannot be traded after the close of trading on the Thursday of expiration week, and the settlement price will be determined the following morning based on the opening price for each stock in the index.

OPTIONS CYCLES

Equity options always have options available for the current month and the following month. In addition, two more months will be available, but those two months will vary, depending on which of three option cycles your option falls within: the January, February, or March quarterly cycles. For an option in the January cycle, Table 1.2 lists Jan, Apr, July, and Oct as the months that will be used. So, in January, the Jan and Feb options (current and next month's) will be available, plus two additional months: Apr and July. By contrast, an option in the February cycle will have the following options available in January: Jan, Feb, May, and Aug. Similarly, an option in the March cycle will have the Jan, Feb, Mar, and Jun options available in January. For stocks without LEAPS options, the Jan options are added in January.

Table 1.3 illustrates how this works for a year with Apple Computer (AAPL) in the January cycle.

This is probably more detail about the option cycles than needed by the average options trader. The key information to keep in mind is that any stock options chain will always have options available for the front month, next month, and two additional months. Those additional months will vary, depending on the option cycle of which it is a member. A smaller subset will also have the LEAPS options available.

TABLE 1.2 Option Cycle Months

Option Cycle	Option Months	LEAPS
January	Jan Apr July Oct	New year added after May expiration
February	Feb May Aug Nov	New year added after June expiration
March	Mar Jun Sep Dec	New year added after July expiration

TABLE 1.3 AAPL Options Available by Month

Front Month	Next Month	Additional Months
Jan	Feb	Apr Jul
Feb	Mar	Apr Jul
Mar	Apr	Jul Oct
Apr	May	Jul Oct
May	Jun	Jul Oct
Jun	Jul	Oct Jan
Jul	Aug	Oct Jan
Aug	Sep	Oct Jan
Sep	Oct	Jan Apr
Oct	Nov	Jan Apr
Nov	Dec	Jan Apr
Dec	Jan	Apr Jul

Index options always have options available for the front month and the following month, but the availability of other options may vary with the product. The specifications for the index option of interest may be found on the web site of the exchange that creates the option. For example, on the International Securities Exchange (ISE) web site at www.ise.com, you will find the specifications for the Standard & Poor's SmallCap 600 Index options (SML). SML always has options available for the three near-term months plus three additional months from the March option cycle.

Next we will consider options pricing. How do I know if an option is expensive or a bargain?

CHAPTER 2

Probability Distributions

E veryday life contains many examples of probabilities. The weather forecast may predict a 40% probability of rain showers for tomorrow. Those of you who have played poker or blackjack are familiar with the probabilities of drawing a particular card to make a hand successful. In this chapter we will briefly explore the mathematics of probabilities that allow us to quantify our expectations of a particular event's occurrence. For options traders, this is critical and foundational information because the pricing of options is rooted in the probabilities of stock price movement.

THE GAUSSIAN DISTRIBUTION

You have probably come across the so-called "bell-shaped curve" either in school or in your business career. Mathematicians refer to this as a *Gaussian distribution* or a *normal distribution*. An example is shown in Figure 2.1. At any point on the curve, the height of the curve gives us the probability of that value's occurring in the population under consideration. It is common for large sets of measurements of many objects to roughly fit the bell-shaped curve of the normal distribution. For example, let's assume I measure the shoe size of every male in the city of Chicago and plot the number of size 9 shoes and the number of size $9\frac{1}{2}$ shoes, and so on until I have a curve similar to Figure 2.1. In this hypothetical example, I measured the largest number of size 11 shoes. Thus, if I were to randomly pick out a man in Chicago, the probability of his having a shoe size of 11 is higher

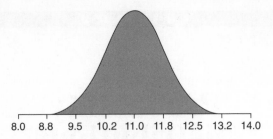

8.0   8.8   9.5   10.2 11.0 11.8 12.5 13.2 14.0

FIGURE 2.1   Example of a Gaussian Distribution

than the probability of his shoe size being 13. You can see how I might use this information to stock the shoes in my athletic shoe store: I would order the largest number of size 11s, somewhat fewer size 10s, and so on.

Mathematicians measure the width of this probability distribution by the standard deviation, commonly denoted by the Greek letter sigma (σ). Distributions with a small standard deviation will be tall and narrow—most of the values are contained in a narrow range around the mean or average value in the center of the curve. Curves with large standard deviations will be lower and very broad; in those cases, there will be higher probabilities of much higher and lower values occurring in that set of data.

The standard deviation also sets some helpful parameters for assessing probabilities. The mean of the probability distribution curve plus or minus one standard deviation ($\pm 1\sigma$) will encompass 68% of the area under the curve. Returning to our shoe size distribution, we have a 68% probability that the man walking into our shoe store in Chicago has a shoe size between 10.25 and 11.75 (11.0 $\pm$ 0.75), where $\sigma = 0.75$ for this distribution. The mean $\pm 2\sigma$ contains 95% of the data, or stated another way, there is a 95% probability that any particular man on the street in Chicago has a shoe size between 9.5 and 12.5 (11.0 $\pm$ 1.50). Similarly, the mean $\pm 3\sigma$, or the area under the curve between 8.75 and 13.25, contains over 99% of the data.

APPLICATION TO THE REAL WORLD

If we use our normal distribution function to predict the probability of a purely random event such as the marble's landing on the black eight of the roulette wheel, we will find a nearly perfect fit to our actual data. And the prediction will be more and more accurate as we spin the roulette wheel more and more times. This is a crucial point of understanding probability distributions: any single trade may not fit the predicted probabilities, but

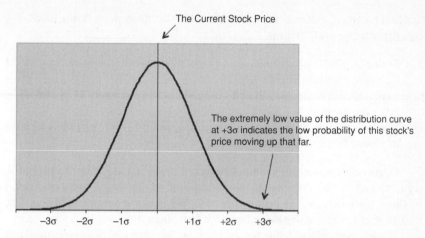

FIGURE 2.2 The Probability Distribution Applied to Stock Prices

over many trades, we will begin to see the actual results converge toward the predicted results.

In Figure 2.2, we have applied this idea of probability distributions to stock prices, where today's stock price is at the center of the curve and there is an equal probability of the stock price's fluctuating up or down by a few points. Imagine that we have a record of this stock's daily price fluctuations for the past couple of years and have computed its volatility, or the average range of its price fluctuations. In this application to stock prices, volatility is the standard deviation for the probability distribution of stock prices. Thus, stocks like Google that may move $10 or $20 in one day have high volatilities and broad probability distributions.

Conversely, stocks like Microsoft have low historical volatility and tall, narrow probability distributions. Figure 2.3 illustrates these principles

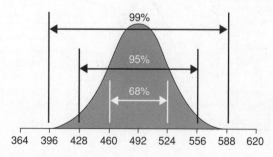

FIGURE 2.3 Probabilities and the Standard Deviation

applied to Google at a price of $492 and a standard deviation of $32. We can draw three conclusions:

- There is a 68% probability of Google's being between $460 and $524 one year from now (±1σ).
- There is a 95% probability of Google's being between $428 and $556 one year from now (±2σ).
- There is a 99% probability of Google's being between $396 and $588 one year from now (±3σ).

One can also use the probability distribution to calculate the probability of Google's being above or below a specified price at a particular point in time; for example, based on this data, we could calculate a probability of 43% that Google will close above $500 in 30 days.

While predictions from the normal probability distribution curves fit randomly generated data very well, they serve only as an approximation to stock price data. The stock market is subject to many nonrandom forces such as rumors, news events, crowd psychology, earnings announcements, and so on. These nonrandom events cause wider fluctuations in stock prices than would be predicted from the model. Figure 2.4 illustrates what is known as the "fat tails problem." If we were to plot the actual prices for a stock over some period of time and compare those prices to the normal probability distribution, we would see a reasonable fit for most of the curve. But out on the extreme edges of the curve, we would observe the deviations noted in Figure 2.4. In the real world, we would see a larger number of ± 3σ moves than we would have predicted based on our probability distribution calculation. Therefore, the curve formed by the actual data would be higher than predicted on the far edges, indicating a higher

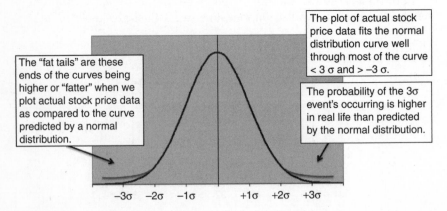

FIGURE 2.4 The Fat Tails Problem

probability of those extreme events occurring; these are the so-called "fat tails" of the curve.

We would be a bit naïve to expect our stock prices to conform perfectly to these probability predictions on any one day or any one trade. But we will find the calculated probabilities to be good estimates of the actual trade outcomes in the long run over many trades.

We will use the probability distributions principally in two ways. The first will be to compare two trade candidates or rank order a series of trade possibilities. Our second use for the probability calculations is to consistently position our income trades each month with respect to the risk of loss. We will cover this application of the probability distribution function in later chapters as we explore income generation trading strategies.

Traders often run various screens to develop trade candidates and then apply quantitative criteria as well as intuitive judgment to narrow the candidates down to the final prospects. Often, that intuitive judgment is based on our observations of the stock's historical price movement. A trader would intuitively know that a $10 move in the price of a hyped-up growth stock is much more likely than a $10 move in a familiar blue-chip stock. Our probability distribution calculations enable us to quantify that comparison and ensure the accuracy of our intuitive judgment.

But our probability calculations have one more valuable lesson for us: risk-adjusted returns, the subject of the next section.

RISK-ADJUSTED RETURNS

We can calculate the probability of a trade's being successful based on the probability of the stock price's being above or below a particular value at some point in time. Assume we are considering a trade that will potentially yield $2,000 in profit or a 15% return on capital at risk, and we have calculated a probability of success of 73%. If we multiply the percentage of the probability of success by the potential return, we will have adjusted the return by the level of risk expected. This is known as the risk-adjusted return (i.e., $0.73 \times 15\% = 11\%$). If we were to execute this trade many times, 11% is the average return we would expect over time. Hence, this is often called the expected return or expected value. But we have not taken the probability of a loss into account; we'll do that with our next example.

Later in this book, we will explore the iron condor spread, one of the more common income generation strategies. The iron condor is often positioned in such a way as to theoretically have an 85% probability of success. We will go through the intricacies of this trade later, but for now, just assume we have an iron condor spread with an 85% probability of a 14% profit of $2,500 and a 15% probability of a 100% loss or $17,500. We can compute our risk-adjusted return over many trades as:

$$\text{Risk-adjusted return} = 0.85(2,500) - 0.15(17,500) = -\$500$$

or

$$\text{Risk-adjusted return} = 0.85(14\%) - 0.15(100\%) = -3\%$$

Therefore, if we establish our iron condor each month with these risk parameters, our risk-adjusted return would be a small net loss after many months of trading. Your first reaction may be that the iron condor isn't a very good strategy and we just need to find a better trading strategy. But, in fact, we will get the same results when we apply these probabilities to any options trading strategy; the risk-adjusted return of any options trading strategy will approach zero over a large number of trades.

In the next chapter, we will discuss the pricing of options and will see that the essence of options pricing is rooted in these same probability distributions we have been exploring in this chapter. The ugly truth is that if options are priced correctly, there is no inherent advantage to holding either side of the trade. *Therefore, the risk-adjusted return of any options strategy will tend toward zero over time.*

Now you may be thinking that you can find the options that are being priced incorrectly by the market and trade those options profitably (e.g., buy cheap options and sell expensive options). That, in fact, is feasible. But this requires you to be able to consistently identify those options and be a better judge of the option's value over time than the collective market. That may be feasible, but it certainly isn't easy. In this book, we will be concentrating on strategies that do not require the trader to predict the direction of the stock or the index, so we will be using the probability distribution calculations primarily to ensure that we are establishing our trades with consistent risk exposure month after month.

We saw above that the risk-adjusted return of any options trading strategy will approach zero over a large number of trades. You might reasonably conclude that it must be impossible to make money by trading options! The answer is yes and no. The risk-adjusted return calculations do in fact tell us that simply putting on an options strategy and allowing it to play out in the market month after month will, in fact, lead to failure. The critical success factor is risk management, a collection of stop losses and adjustment techniques that allow us to manage the trade and basically alter the risk-adjusted return equation.

If I applied risk management to the iron condor strategy discussed earlier and could ensure that my worst loss would be double my maximum profit, or $5,000 (a 29% loss), then my risk-adjusted return equations shift dramatically:

$$\text{Risk adjusted return} = 0.85(2,500) - 0.15(5,000) = \$1,375$$

or

$$\text{Risk-adjusted return} = 0.85(14\%) - 0.15(29\%) = +8\%$$

So now we have an options trading strategy that is expected over time to average 8% returns monthly. In fact, many traders manage the iron condor strategy even better than this example would suggest. But a steady return of 8% per month is huge!

Articles, books, and classes on options trading have tended to emphasize the author's or instructor's favorite strategy and often suggest they have discovered the "Holy Grail" of trading or the one true way to make money by trading options. The truth is, as illustrated above:

The risk-adjusted return of any options strategy will tend toward zero over time.

These Holy Grail trading strategies tend to fall into two extreme categories. One will be advertised as a high-probability trading system; the other will usually be advertised as a low-risk trading system, but it really should be more accurately named a low-probability trading system. Let's compare these alternative approaches and see if either one has an inherent advantage.

HIGH-PROBABILITY TRADING

The essence of this trading philosophy is to develop trades where the probability of success is quite high; it is often marketed as "put the odds on your side." The iron condor spread we described earlier would be an example where our probability of success is 85% or higher (if you aren't familiar with iron condors, don't be concerned; we will explore these strategies in more detail later).

We expected our iron condor strategy to gain $2,500 each month with an 85% probability, but take a complete loss about 15% of the time. Figure 2.5 illustrates the fundamental nature of this trade over time. As you can see, even though we don't lose very often, our losses wipe out all of our gains. This figuratively illustrates the results of our risk-adjusted return equations; over time, the high-probability trading strategy loses money or breaks even at best.

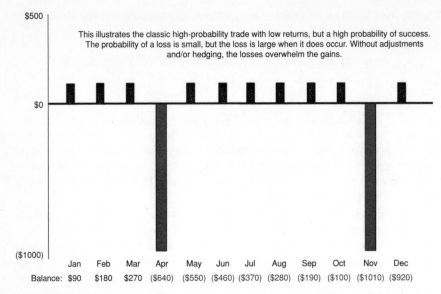

This illustrates the classic high-probability trade with low returns, but a high probability of success. The probability of a loss is small, but the loss is large when it does occur. Without adjustments and/or hedging, the losses overwhelm the gains.

	Jan	Feb	Mar	Apr	May	Jun	Jul	Aug	Sep	Oct	Nov	Dec
Balance:	$90	$180	$270	($640)	($550)	($460)	($370)	($280)	($190)	($100)	($1010)	($920)

FIGURE 2.5   Gain/Loss Patterns of High-Probability Strategies

Most people consider these types of trades to be conservative strategies because of the high probability of success. But the Achilles' heel is the large loss that is possible, even though the probability of its occurrence is low. High-probability trades are feasible only when coupled with robust risk management systems for controlling and minimizing the losses. Then and only then can one enjoy a trading strategy with an expectation of positive returns over time.

LOW-PROBABILITY TRADING

Proponents of low-probability trading usually emphasize that a relatively small investment is required for this type of trade and therefore market this approach as a low-risk trading strategy. A common rule of thumb from the proponents of this approach is to insist that you should trade only when the potential return is two to three times the potential loss. These trades are rarely called low-probability trades because that wouldn't be good marketing. The lottery ticket available in most states is an extreme illustration of the low-risk trade. The investment is small, but the probability of success is extremely small.

In options strategies, the best example of a low-probability trade is an out-of-the-money (OTM) vertical spread. Again, the name of the trade is irrelevant at this point; focus on the potential gains, potential losses, and the relative probabilities of those occurrences. For this type of trade to be successful, the stock price must dramatically rise during the time of the trade; of course, this is a low-probability event. A typical OTM vertical spread might have a 27% probability of achieving a gain of $650 or 185%, versus a potential loss of $350 with a probability of 67% (I have simplified this example by ignoring the probability of the price landing within the spread so the probabilities do not sum to 100%). Our risk-adjusted returns are computed as:

$$\text{Risk-adjusted return} = 0.27(650) - 0.67(350) = -\$59$$

or

$$\text{Risk-adjusted return} = 0.27(185\%) - 0.67(100\%) = -17\%$$

If we traded this strategy consistently over time, we would expect a pattern of wins and losses similar to that illustrated in Figure 2.6.

With the low-probability trading strategy, we have frequent small losses and occasional large gains, but the losses add up and overwhelm the gains over time. So we have a similar result here as we saw with high-probability trades. Low-probability trades are feasible only when coupled with robust risk management systems for controlling and minimizing the

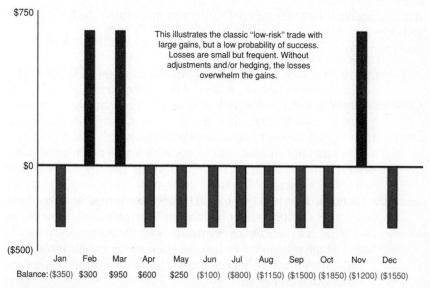

FIGURE 2.6 Gain/Loss Patterns of Low-Probability Strategies

losses. However, risk management of these trades is even more difficult in practice due to the small initial investment; various risk management techniques would be hard pressed to preserve much of the initial investment and yet allow the trader to stay in enough trades to enjoy the rare large gain. That is the essence of why we will be concentrating our attention on high-probability trades for consistent income generation.

Many options trading myths have developed out of a basic misunderstanding of the probabilities associated with options trading. We will explore these myths in the next section.

OPTIONS TRADING MYTHS

The purpose of establishing this foundation of probability distributions and risk-adjusted returns is to give you a firm foundation for trading options. Many people have been misinformed about options trading and this has led to unrealistic expectations. Unfortunately, this has often led to significant losses in the markets. The marketing hype is simply that, but that doesn't mean you cannot succeed in options trading. Let's debunk some myths before we continue the journey.

"You should place low risk/reward trades only where you are risking $1 to make $3."

But the probability of earning that $3 profit is very low. Over time, the losses will overwhelm your infrequent gains.

"A far out-of-the-money (OTM) bull call spread is a low-risk trade because we are risking only $1."

Only $1 is at risk, but the probability of losing that $1 is quite high. This is the options equivalent of the lottery ticket.

"If I position an iron condor trade with an 85% probability of success, I will make a profit 10 months out of the year, have only two losing months, and therefore be profitable for the year."

A high probability of success comes with a high risk/reward ratio; therefore, the losses of those two losing months will wipe out the year's gains.

"I always trade deep in-the-money (ITM) bull call spreads where I am making only a 10% profit but I have a 90% probability of success. This is a conservative strategy that almost always makes money."

Again, a high probability of success comes with a high risk/reward ratio; losses will be infrequent but large. Over time, the net returns will tend toward zero.

"You should only sell options because most options expire worthless." The probability of the option's expiring worthless is built into the option's price. There is no inherent advantage to taking either side of this trade.

"You should only buy options because you have limited downside risk." The probability of a long option's ultimately being profitable is built into the option's price. There is no inherent advantage to taking either side of this trade.

One of the most important lessons of applying probability distribution calculations to our trading is to debunk the common marketing hype of options trading, namely, that the iron condor or broken-wing butterfly or whatever is the best trading strategy. The harsh reality is that there is no such thing as a "best options strategy." The risk-adjusted return of any options strategy will tend toward zero over time.

Understanding the probabilities underlying our trade enables us to predict the expected pattern of results of gains and losses. A robust risk management system is crucial for the long-term success and profitability of any options trading strategy.

WHAT IS A CONSERVATIVE TRADE?

One final point of terminology remains before we move on to options pricing. What constitutes a *conservative* trade?

Generally, in the world of finance, a conservative investment is one with minimal volatility, highly predictable returns, and a very low probability of loss. However, as we have seen above, this isn't true in the world of options trading. Options are a probabilistic investment. The options strategies with high probabilities of success have a dark side: the large loss with a low probability of occurrence; it may be infrequent, but when it occurs, it is devastating.

Conservative options trading strategies are those with high probabilities of success. But don't be deceived. This is nothing like a conservative investment in Treasury bonds. These conservative strategies must be properly managed to avoid significant losses. Risk management is the essential key to success and we will be emphasizing it throughout this book.

The Las Vegas casino is an excellent metaphor for our options trading education. If you owned a casino and saw someone winning a bundle at one of your tables, you wouldn't be concerned because you know the odds are in your favor. There is a small probabilistic advantage built into all of the games. Over time and many plays, the house must win. The casino owner knows he has an edge.

Many retail traders approach options trading like the player sitting at the Las Vegas casino table. The trader gets excited after earning over 100% on one trade and tells all of his friends. But over time and many trades, he is losing money. The odds are stacked against him, just as we saw when we calculated the risk-adjusted returns for some options trading strategies in the sections above.

Your model for trading options should be the casino owner, not the player at the tables. You must develop a system of trading and risk management rules and follow them with great discipline. If you understand the probabilities underlying the particular strategy being employed, and you have ensured that your trading system gives you that probabilistic edge, you are now trading like the casino, not the player sitting at one of the tables. Incorporating risk management into your trading system gives you the edge.

EXERCISES

You may find a probability calculator on your brokerage web site or download one from my web site: www.ParkwoodCapitalLLC.com.

1. GOOG closed today at $353.02, with only one day left in October's options. Implied volatility (IV) of the Oct $350 call option is 241%. GOOG will announce earnings after the close.

   a. Calculate the probability of the Oct $350 call's expiring ITM (i.e., with the stock price > $350).

   b. Assume you are very bullish on GOOG; what is the probability of GOOG's closing by expiration above $400?

   c. We would have to pay $7 or $700 for one contract of the Oct $400 calls. What will these calls be worth on expiration Friday (tomorrow) if GOOG closes at $408?

   d. Why is the implied volatility so high?

   e. True or false: This extremely high IV means the market thinks GOOG is going much higher.

   f. What price range for GOOG would you predict for tomorrow with a 68% probability?

2. IBM is trading at $91.52, IV = 63%, and Nov options have 36 days to expiration. We buy a $70/$80 bull call spread for $8.80. Our maximum profit of $1.20 will occur if IBM closes on expiration Friday above

$80. Our maximum loss of $8.80 will occur if IBM closes on expiration Friday below $70.

   a. What is the probability of success for this trade?
   b. What is the probability of the maximum loss occurring?
   c. If you were to place a trade similar to this on IBM every month for a year, how many months would you predict you would be successful?
   d. Would you expect to be profitable at the end of the year? Why or why not?

3. XOM is trading at $69.45, IV = 83%, and Nov options have 36 days to expiration. We buy an $80/$90 bull call spread for $1.57. Our maximum profit of $8.43 will occur if XOM closes on expiration Friday above $90. Our maximum loss of $1.57 will occur if XOM closes on expiration Friday below $80.

   a. What is the probability of success for this trade?
   b. What is the probability of a maximum loss occurring?
   c. If you were to place a trade similar to this on XOM every month for a year, how many months would you predict you would be successful?

4. Compare and contrast the IBM and XOM trades in questions 2 and 3. Which trade is best? Why?

5. One of your friends tells you he is trading a very conservative options strategy that has a 90% probability of success, so he has cashed in his entire stock portfolio to invest in this strategy because he "can't lose." Without even knowing the details of the options strategy, what can you tell your friend about the likely outcomes of this strategy over time?

6. We are considering three trades:

   (1) IBM is trading at $118, IV = 23%, and we have 46 days to expiration of the October options. We are considering a spread where IBM must close above $130 at expiration to make 400% on the trade.
   (2) BAC is trading at $18, IV = 49%, and we have 46 days to expiration of the October options. We are considering a spread where BAC must close above $25 at expiration to make 1,037% on the trade.
   (3) AIG is trading at $45, IV = 152%, and we have 46 days to expiration of the October options. We are considering a spread where AIG must close above $55 at expiration to make 213% on the trade.

   a. Compute the expected return for each proposed trade.
   b. Which trade would you consider best and why?

CHAPTER 3

Options Pricing and Implied Volatility

One of the most fundamental questions for any investment concerns the price. Is it too expensive, or is it a bargain? In stock investments, one turns to price-to-earnings ratios, earnings growth rates, book values, and other measures to determine a stock's worth. In 1973, Fisher Black and Myron Scholes published a theoretical model to price equity options. Robert Merton built upon that original paper with his work and was the first to refer to the pricing equation as the "Black-Scholes" options pricing model. In 1997, Merton and Scholes won the Nobel Prize in economics for this achievement. (Fisher Black was not eligible since he had died in 1995). This equation enabled investors to compute a quantitative measure of an option's value and spurred the beginning of options trading on a large public scale. The Chicago Board Options Exchange was founded in 1973 and the Options Clearing Corporation began in 1977.

THE BLACK-SCHOLES PRICING MODEL

The Black-Scholes options pricing model is rather complex, but the calculations have been done for us on our brokerage platforms and in the options analysis software that is widely available. My point in displaying it here is to illustrate the relationships of the variables in the equation. The Black-Scholes pricing model calculates the price of a call option as (a similar equation calculates the put value):

$$P_c = s\phi(d_1) - xe^{-rt}\phi(d_2)$$

where P_c = the calculated, or theoretical, price of the call option
        $d_1 = [\log(s/x) + (r + \sigma^2/2)t]/[\sigma\sqrt{t}]$
        $d_2 = d_1 - \sigma\sqrt{t}$
        s = the stock price
        x = the strike price
        r = the interest rate
        t = time in years until option expiration
        σ = historical volatility
        ϕ = the normal cumulative probability distribution function

Don't be put off by the complexity of this equation. I have included it in this chapter for completeness and to clearly show the relationship between options pricing and the probability distributions we discussed in the previous chapter. Focus on the key components of the equation, how they interact with each other, and how the option price will be affected by these other variables. Notice what a prominent role the probability distribution function (ϕ) plays in this pricing model; the pricing of options is fundamentally rooted in the probabilities discussed in the previous chapter. This is one of the primary differences between trading options and trading stocks.

The option price depends on several variables: the stock price, the strike price, the interest rate, time to expiration, and the stock's historical volatility. Of all of these variables, the interest rate is the least important for options with reasonably short-term expirations. However, the interest rate becomes more important when calculating the value of Long-Term Equity Anticipation Securities (LEAPS) options, with expirations up to two years. In most cases, the infrequent and small changes in interest rates together with the low dependence of the Black-Scholes equation on the interest rate cause investors to generally ignore interest rates when calculating theoretical option prices.

THE GREEKS

The Greeks are quantitative measures of the sensitivity of the option's theoretical price to the several variables in the Black-Scholes model. Differential calculus allows us to determine the sensitivity of our calculated option price to changes in individual variables of the equation, such as the stock price, while holding all other variables constant. Don't panic if your calculus is rusty. All of the math has been done for you. These mathematical derivatives are called the Greeks in options trading because a Greek letter is used to represent them.

Let's look at the big picture first before diving into the details of the Greeks. Consider the relationships of the variables in the Black-Scholes equation in broad, qualitative terms. The larger the separation is between the current stock price and the strike price, the smaller the option's price will become. Recalling the probability distribution's shape, this makes sense. There is a smaller probability of a price's occurrence as we move away from the peak of the distribution. This relationship of the option price and the stock price will be represented in quantitative terms by the Greek delta (Δ), discussed later in this chapter.

We would expect the price of an option to be higher, as we have more time available for our prediction to come true. In general, longer-term options will be more expensive. This relationship of time to the price of the option is represented by the Greek theta (θ). Theta measures the change in the option price due to the passage of one day of time while all other variables are held constant. Theta values for individual options are always negative.

If we were considering the purchase of an option on a stock that is highly volatile, with frequent large price moves, we would not be surprised to find that that option was more expensive than the option of a slow-moving blue-chip stock. This relationship of volatility to the option price is represented by the Greek *vega*. Highly volatile stocks have more expensive options. Vega is unique among the Greeks in that it is not actually a Greek letter. Most commonly, it is represented by a capital V. Some academic literature will use kappa (κ) as the Greek letter associated with the volatility sensitivity of the Black-Scholes equation.

Rho (ρ) measures the sensitivity of the option price to changes in the interest rate. Generally, changes in interest rates have a negligible effect on the commonly traded options of a few weeks or months in duration.

Gamma (γ) is unique among the Greeks in that it measures the change in one of the Greeks with a change in the stock price; gamma measures the change in delta with a $1 change in the stock price. Gamma is a measure of sensitivity for delta.

We will explore the Greeks in more depth later in this chapter.

IMPLIED VOLATILITY

If we enter all the appropriate data into the Black-Scholes equation and calculate the option price, we may see a discrepancy with the actual market price for that option. The market price may be higher or lower than the calculated or theoretical option price, but more often it is higher. The only variable in the Black-Scholes equation that might account for this discrepancy is the historical volatility. If we enter the market price of the option into the Black-Scholes equation and calculate volatility, the result is the volatility "implied" by the market price, or *implied volatility*. If the market price was higher than the theoretical price, then implied volatility was higher than the historical volatility. The marketplace has priced this option higher because they expect the price volatility of this stock to be higher than it has been in the past. Thus, implied volatility is a measure of the market's consensus estimate of future volatility for this stock.

We may also consider implied volatility as a measure of price risk. Consider the situation where we are contemplating an investment in two different stocks, both priced at $50 per share, but one with an implied volatility of 20% and the other at 85%. The lower-volatility stock has a 68% probability of being between $47 and $53 in 30 days, but the higher-volatility stock could close at prices within $38 and $62 (plus or minus one standard deviation). The investor who buys the high-volatility stock must be prepared for wider swings in the price of his investment.

Option prices may vary widely due to swings in implied volatility. For this reason, some traders follow a small number of stocks and track their historical fluctuation in implied volatility. They will buy options when implied volatility is low and sell options when implied volatility is high. As implied volatility returns to its norm, these option positions will tend to appreciate in value.

Implied volatility is also the reason many beginning options traders are surprised when their option position loses value or remains unchanged even though the trader's prediction for the price of the underlying stock was correct. A decrease in implied volatility will cause the option price to decrease and may overwhelm the increase in the call option's price due to the rising stock price, or the increase in the put option's price due to the falling stock price.

BUILDING THE PRICE OF AN OPTION

An option's market price is composed of three quantities: intrinsic or real value, time to expiration, and implied volatility. Often, you will read that the option price consists of intrinsic and extrinsic value, where extrinsic value includes time and implied volatility. I prefer to separate out the effects of time and implied volatility, but, as we will see, it is difficult to precisely separate the value due to time from the value due to implied volatility.

The intrinsic value of an option is the value of that option if I were to exercise it today. Thus, a $200 call option for Apple Computer is worth $11 when Apple is selling for $211 because we could exercise our call and buy

100 shares of Apple at $200 per share, sell it for $211 per share, and have a profit of $11 per share. However, the market price of that call option is probably much higher than $11 because the market price also accounts for how much time is left until expiration as well as the implied volatility of Apple at this time.

A $200 call option for Apple with 12 days to expiration may be selling for $12.50, but another $200 call option for Apple with 47 days to expiration is selling for $18.45. Assuming the implied volatility of the two options is identical, the difference of $5.95 is due to the additional 35 days of time.

Continuing with this same example of Apple Computer, the market price for the $230 call option with 47 days to expiration is $5.45. In this case, the intrinsic value is zero; if we were to exercise the $230 call and buy Apple stock at $230 while Apple is trading at $211, we would lose money. So we would not exercise the call because the intrinsic value is zero. The market price of the $230 call consists of only time value and implied volatility. If we compare the $230 call option with 47 days to expiration, selling for $5.45, to the $230 call option with 12 days to expiration, selling for $0.79, we see that the difference for the 35 days of time is $4.66. The difference in the $200 call option prices was $5.95 for the two different expirations. We would expect the time value to be very similar, so the implied volatility of the two $230 call options must be different. This is an example of a volatility skew, where the implied volatility differs for two different months of options. This frequently occurs when an earnings announcement is scheduled for next month. The implied volatility of next month's options will be higher than the current month due to the market's expectations for a large price move following the announcement. But note that increased implied volatility does not suggest a particular directional move; it only suggests the increased probability of a larger price move than usual for this stock; the price move could be up or down.

The market price of any option consists of its intrinsic value, the time remaining to expiration, and implied volatility. The price of the option will increase as the option has more intrinsic value, more time to expiration, and higher implied volatility.

A CLOSER LOOK AT THE GREEKS

Each of the Greeks is an expression of the sensitivity of the option's price to one of the variables in the Black-Scholes equation, assuming all other variables are held constant. Delta (Δ) measures how much the option price will change with a $1 move in the underlying stock or index price. Delta is commonly represented in different ways. A delta of $0.56 indicates the call option value will increase by $0.56 if the stock price increases by $1. You may see this delta value listed as 0.56, 56, or 56%. Delta values of calls are always positive, whereas the deltas of puts are always negative; that is, the put value decreases with an increase in stock price. We will explore the use of delta in our trading later, but for now, think of delta as a measure of the price risk of our position. As delta becomes a larger positive or negative number, our option position gains or loses more money with changes in the stock price. Delta increases as the option moves in-the-money (ITM) and approaches 1.00 or 100. Conversely, as the option moves out-of-the-money (OTM), delta decreases and approaches zero. Delta increases with more time to expiration.

Gamma (γ) measures how much the value of delta will change with a $1 move in the underlying stock or index price. Larger values of gamma are warning us that price changes in the underlying stock or index price are going to have greater and greater effects on delta. For example, if gamma = 0.05 and delta = 0.50 and the stock price increases by $1.50, the call option price will increase by $0.75 (1.5 × 0.50), but the next one-dollar increase in the stock price will increase the call option price by $0.55 (0.50 + 0.05). Gamma is larger at-the-money (ATM) and decreases as we move farther ITM or OTM. Gamma also increases as we near expiration. Large values of gamma are the reason ATM option positions can change value rapidly during the week of expiration. This is the underlying theoretical basis for the trading system rules that often call for closing positions on the Friday before expiration week.

The price of an option decreases over time with all other variables held constant. The Greek theta (θ) measures the value of the option's time value that is lost with the passage of one day in time. Theta is always a negative value and is larger as we approach expiration. When we own an option (called being *long* the option), the passage of time always hurts us by decreasing the value of the option we own. When I make a price prediction for a stock and purchase an option on that stock, my position will lose value each day if nothing changes except the passage of time. However, when we have sold the option (referred to as being *short* the option), theta is now positive so our position gains in value as time passes, assuming all other factors are held constant. The options trading strategies often used for income generation benefit from the passage of time; they are positive theta positions. When we are trading those kinds of strategies, we attempt to maximize theta for our position. The passage of time is our friend with positive theta positions.

Vega (V) measures the sensitivity of our option or our option position to changes in implied volatility. Increases in implied volatility increase the price of options and decreases in implied volatility decrease the price of options. Values of vega increase with more time to expiration, are highest

ATM, and decrease toward zero as we move farther OTM or farther ITM. As we develop more complex option positions in later chapters, we will examine the vega value for the overall position as a measure of the position's exposure to large moves in implied volatility.

HOW WILL WE USE THE GREEKS?

As we discuss specific options strategies throughout the rest of this book, we will show how we use the Greeks to manage that particular trade. In general, the Greeks are useful in two ways:

1. To evaluate and compare several trade candidates
2. To manage the ongoing trade and determine appropriate adjustments when necessary

The software on your brokerage web site will compute the position Greeks for you. If you were calculating the Greeks manually, you would sum the individual option Greeks, taking care to multiply by the number of contracts and changing the sign of options sold. If one trade has a much larger delta value than another, then that trade is much more bullish if the delta is positive, or much more bearish if the position delta is negative. Your position delta specifies the price risk for this position. A position delta of $125 tells us that if the underlying index or stock price decreases by $5 tomorrow, and all other variables are held constant, our position will decrease in value by $625.

Large vega values for a position warn us that this position is sensitive to changes in implied volatility. Thus, large positive vega trades will gain in value with increasing implied volatility and lose value as implied volatility decreases. Positions with large negative values of vega lose value when implied volatility increases. Traders refer to positions with large positive or large negative values of vega as having "vega risk."

The value of theta for our position specifies our sensitivity to the passage of time. Positions with negative theta will slowly lose value with the passage of time if nothing else changes. When I buy a call option based on my prediction that the stock price will increase, I have a negative theta position. If the stock price simply trades sideways, my position will steadily lose value due to what we refer to as time decay or theta decay. Many of the income strategies we will discuss in later chapters benefit from time decay; they are positive theta positions that gain in value with the passage of time (again, assuming all other variables stay constant).

As we discuss various options trading strategies in future chapters, we will use the Greeks of the positions to evaluate the trade-offs and sensitivities to market conditions and use this to help us make the optimal choice of trading strategy given our assessment of market conditions.

Once a trade position has been established, we will look to the Greeks of the position to assess our ongoing risk. Those Greek values will trigger our decisions to close the trade and/or make adjustments to the position.

This chapter covered the factors that influence the pricing of an option and introduced the Greeks, quantitative measures of the sensitivity of the option price to changes in variables such as stock price, implied volatility, and time. The practical utility of the Greeks will become clearer as we discuss the use and management of more complex options trading strategies in later chapters.

EXERCISES

1. What do we normally use the Black-Scholes equation to calculate?
2. Explain the difference between historical volatility and implied volatility.
3. If the Market Volatility Index (VIX) is higher than it has been in the past 12 months, what does that tell me?
4. An option's price has three components. Name them and explain how they fluctuate in the market.
5. Define the Greeks: delta, gamma, vega, and theta.
6. What does it mean if my position delta is +$105?
7. If implied volatility is at historically high levels, would I want my position vega to be positive or negative? Why?
8. When is theta positive and when is it negative?
9. If I own an ATM call option and the underlying stock price and implied volatility remain unchanged, will my position's value be increased, decreased, or unchanged? Why?

CHAPTER 4

Vertical Spreads

O ption spreads are created when we buy one option and simultaneously sell another option. When the two options are within the same expiration month, the spread is known as a *vertical* spread. The vertical spread derives its name from the early days of options trading when the prices were posted on a wall with the strike prices listed vertically and the different expiration months listed horizontally across the top. Spreads created by buying and selling options within the same expiration month, or from the same vertical column, were called vertical spreads.

Later in this book we will discuss calendar spreads, wherein one buys an option in a future month and sells the option in the front month at the same strike price. The older name for this spread is a *horizontal* spread due to the positions of the options on the board: both in the same row (same strike price) but in different columns (different expiration months).

Vertical spreads are useful tools for the trader to profit from her prediction of a stock's price move. But it is also important to fully understand the intricacies of vertical spreads because they form the building blocks for more complex options strategies such as the condor and butterfly spreads.

BUILDING THE VERTICAL SPREAD

Let's start with an example of a vertical spread. With IBM trading at $126, we buy an IBM $120 Feb call for $6.43 or $643 for one contract. I can then create a spread by selling the IBM $130 Feb call for $0.75 or $75. I have

33

created the IBM 120/130 call spread for $568. If IBM closes at February expiration above $130 per share, then the person I sold the $130 call option to will exercise that call, requiring me to sell 100 shares of IBM stock at $130 per share. But I will exercise my $120 call and buy 100 shares of IBM at $120 per share and then use those shares to satisfy the $130 call exercised against me. That leaves me with $1,000 in my account. I spent $568 establishing the trade so my net profit is $432.

This vertical spread is often called a *bull call* spread, since it is built with calls and would be used when you have a bullish expectation for a stock; in this example, IBM was trading at $126 and we expected it to move above $130 during the next month. We may also create a bullish vertical spread with puts on IBM by buying the $120 Feb put for $0.86 and selling the $130 Feb put for $5.26. In this case, we received more for the option we sold than for the option we purchased, so we have a net cash flow into our account, or a credit of $440. For this spread, the maximum profit is attained when IBM closes above $130 at expiration and both put options expire worthless. The original credit of $440 is our profit. This vertical put spread is often called a *bull put* spread.

When the option we sold is priced higher than the option we bought, we have created a *credit* spread. When the option we bought is more costly than the option we sold, we have a net cash flow out of our account, or a debit; we have created a *debit* spread. Often traders will say they have "bought a call spread," meaning they built a debit spread with calls. The above IBM example with puts would be called "selling a put spread" or establishing a bull put spread. This terminology is summarized in Table 4.1.

Let's return to our first example of the IBM Feb 120/130 bull call spread. This spread could be established for a debit of $568 for one contract. The maximum loss for any debit spread is simply the original debit. The maximum profit for any debit spread is found by subtracting the debit from the value of the spread; if the two strike prices of the spread are $10 apart, the spread value is $1,000; if $5 apart, then the value is $500 and so on. For this example, the maximum profit is $432 (1,000 − 568) and the return is 76% (profit divided by the capital at risk or 432/568).

TABLE 4.1 Vertical Spread Terminology

Calls or Puts in Spread	Posture	Retail Name	Pit Name	Credit or Debit
Calls	Bullish	Bull call spread	Buying a call spread	Debit
Calls	Bearish	Bear call spread	Selling a call spread	Credit
Puts	Bullish	Bull put spread	Selling a put spread	Credit
Puts	Bearish	Bear put spread	Buying a put spread	Debit

TABLE 4.2 Vertical Spread Return Calculations

Debit or Credit Spread	Maximum Profit	Maximum Loss	% Return
Debit	Spread – Debit	Debit	[(Spread – Debit)/ Debit] × 100
Credit	Credit	Spread – Credit	[Credit/(Spread – Credit)] × 100

The IBM Feb 120/130 bull put spread could be established for a credit of $440 so the maximum potential profit is the credit or $440 and the maximum potential loss is the spread less the credit or $560. The potential return is 78%.

Notice that the debit call spread has approximately the same return as the credit spread at the same strike prices. So there is no inherent advantage to using the debit spread or the credit spread to profit from your bullish prediction. The choice of a credit or a debit spread is principally one of style preference. The profit and loss calculations for vertical spreads are summarized in Table 4.2.

EFFECTS OF IMPLIED VOLATILITY

One of the commonly repeated myths associated with options trading is, "When implied volatility is high, sell credit spreads, and when implied volatility is low, buy debit spreads." In this section we will show why that statement isn't true, but that doesn't mean implied volatility (IV) has no effect on a vertical spread.

We saw in our examples with IBM in the previous section that the returns of the bullish credit spread and the bullish debit spread, placed at the same strike prices, were virtually identical. Consider two more examples from September 29, 2009. Simple Technology (STEC) was trading at $30.11 and its IV was 83%, which was at the 91st percentile of its IV history. The November $25/$30 bull call spread would have cost $300 and would have returned 67% if STEC closed over $30 at November expiration. However, when we looked at the Nov $25/$30 bull put spread, we found it would have brought in a credit of $205 and therefore could have returned 69% if successful. Thus, the credit and debit spreads at the same strikes for a very high IV stock had virtually identical returns.

Let's consider a low IV example from the same period of time. On September 29, 2009, Netflix (NFLX) was trading at $47.16 and had an IV of

44%, which was in its 18th percentile historically. The November $40/$45 bull call spread would have cost $370 to establish and would have returned a maximum of 35%. If the myth were true, this debit spread should have the superior return, but the November $40/$45 bull put spread would have brought in a credit of $125 and therefore had a maximum potential return of 33%. Again, we see the same result. The credit and debit spreads at the same strike prices for a low-IV stock had virtually identical returns.

Vertical spreads are the option investment vehicle of choice in a high-volatility environment when buying the individual option would be very expensive. Since we are both buying and selling the high-IV options, the effects of the high volatility effectively cancel out. But what happens if IV changes while we are in the vertical spread position?

Recall how the spread makes its profit. When we establish a credit spread with a $10 spread in strike prices and the options expire worthless, we simply keep the credit we received initially—no more and no less. Similarly, both options of the debit spread will expire in the money so they will both be exercised, leaving the value of the spread, or $1,000 in the account (for a $10 spread). The difference between the original debit and the spread value is the maximum profit. High or low IV can't change those facts. But it does affect the value of our spread during the interim before expiration.

Figure 4.1 shows the risk/reward graph for a Google (GOOG) $490/$500 bull put spread in August 2008 with GOOG at $491. The initial credit was $5,300 and the maximum loss was $4,700. The heavy black line is the value of the position at expiration as a function of varying stock prices. The value of the spread varies with time to expiration, IV, and the price of the underlying stock. Of course, interest rates and dividends will also affect spread values, but these will be less significant effects. The other curves show the value of the spread with decreasing time to expiration. These time decay curves show quantitatively what spread traders observe every day; that is, the underlying stock price may have moved as predicted above or below the spread strike prices, but the spread cannot be closed for a value close to the maximum theoretical profit until close to expiration. The value of the spread will gradually approach the maximum profit as the time value of the options decays to zero.

Increasing IV during the trade results in the time decay curves being flattened toward an imaginary diagonal line drawn between the maximum gain and maximum loss limits of the trade (imagine the time decay curve for today in Figure 4.1 as a string and we pull it taut). The practical effect for the trader is that the value of the spread approaches the ultimate value at expiration more slowly. Therefore, the probability of closing the trade early for a majority of the maximum profit is reduced. Figure 4.2 shows the risk graph for our GOOG credit spread assuming IV has

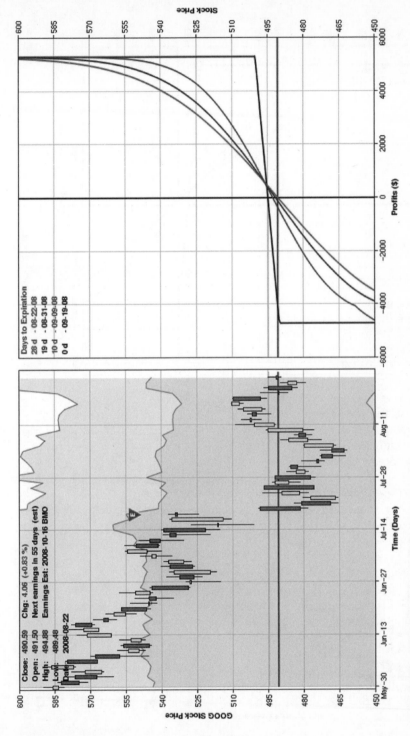

FIGURE 4.1 Risk/Reward Graph for GOOG Bull Put Spread

Source: Screenshots provided courtesy of Optionetics Platinum © 2010. All rights reserved, etc.

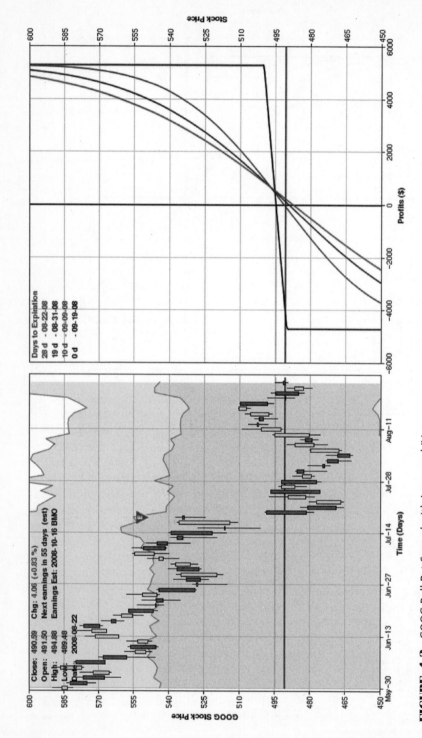

FIGURE 4.2 GOOG Bull Put Spread with Increased IV

Source: Screenshots provided courtesy of Optionetics Platinum © 2010. All rights reserved, etc.

continually increased over the life of the trade, ending at a value 50% higher at expiration.

Note how the time decay curve for the first day of the trade at 28 days to expiration is nearly superimposed on the line for 19 days to expiration. Therefore, nine days would elapse and the value of our trade would change very little. Also note how the line at 10 days to expiration has pulled away from the day of expiration curve (the heavy black line). In practical terms, what this shows is that closing the trade with 10 days to expiration would achieve less of the potential profit if IV has increased during the trade. However, the maximum profit at expiration is unchanged by the increased IV. You just have to remain in the trade longer to receive it.

The flattening effect on the time decay curves due to increasing IV during the life of the trade is identical for credit and debit vertical spreads. Therefore, if one is expecting a large IV increase, such as in advance of an earnings announcement, there is no inherent advantage to either a credit or a debit spread. But one should expect to have to carry the trade closer to expiration to achieve a majority of the potential profit if IV increases.

In Figure 4.1 we see that we could expect to close the trade for a profit of $2,800 at ten days to expiration with GOOG at $510. Note how this expectation is reduced in Figure 4.2 to approximately $2,000 with an increase in IV. But we would still achieve the maximum gain at expiration for GOOG at $510.

Figure 4.3 displays the risk/reward curves for this same GOOG $490/$500 bull put spread with IV decreased by 50% during the life of the trade. Decreasing IV resulted in the time decay curves spreading out toward the curve at expiration and increases the separation between the individual curves. The practical effect for the trader is that the value of the spread approaches the ultimate value at expiration more quickly. Therefore, the probability of closing the trade early for a majority of the maximum profit is increased. Now we see that we could close the trade with ten days to expiration for a gain of about $4,200 with GOOG at $510, or about double the return in the increased IV case of Figure 4.2. However, in both cases, the return for GOOG at $510 at expiration would be identical at $5,300.

Changes in IV during the time we are in a vertical spread will affect the proportion of the profit available to us if we wish to close the trade early, but it does not affect the ultimate profitability at expiration. Thus, we say that vertical spreads are negative vega positions; that is, increasing IV will decrease the position value and decreasing IV will increase the position's value. But the ultimate profitability of the spread at expiration is not affected by changes in IV.

The myth of using credit spreads when IV is high and debit spreads when IV is low may be a confusion that arose out of long and short option

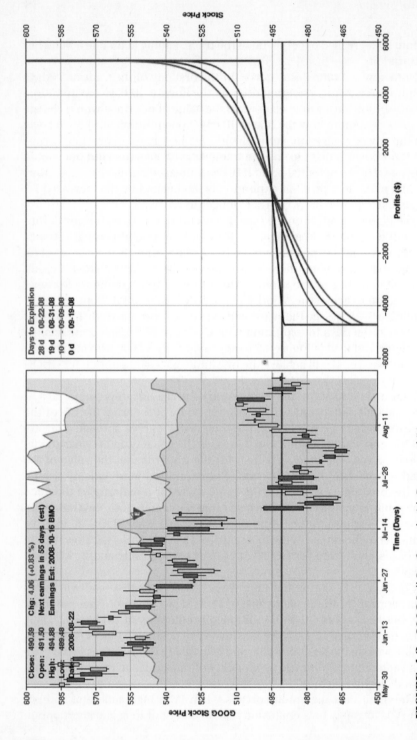

FIGURE 4.3 GOOG Bull Put Spread with Decreased IV

Source: Screenshots provided courtesy of Optionetics Platinum © 2010. All rights reserved, etc.

40

positions. It is indeed true that one should consider buying low-volatility options and selling high-volatility options. If we are considering a long call or put position, we would look for options with low IV because these are inexpensive options. And similarly, we would target high-IV options if we were considering a short call or put position.

However, when playing the stock's directional move with a vertical spread strategy, the choice of a credit or debit spread is largely a personal preference. Some prefer a credit spread because they can earn interest on the credit monies in their accounts while in the trade; another advantage of credit spreads is fewer trading commissions (assuming the spread is allowed to expire worthless). Others prefer debit spreads because they have spent the maximum that can be lost on the trade; there is no possibility of an ugly surprise later if the trade turns against them (as there is for a credit spread).

The returns for credit and debit spreads will be identical, and IV levels will have no effect on the returns. The effect of the volatility (either high or low) effectively cancels itself out by the opposite nature of the two legs of the spread. Thus, vertical spreads are an excellent way to trade high-volatility options when establishing a long option position would be both expensive and risky.

EARLY EXERCISE

All stock options may be exercised on any business day prior to expiration. These are known as *American-style* options. *European-style* options can be exercised only at expiration. Most, but not all, broad index options are European style (e.g., SPX, RUT, NDX, and others). But the OEX (Standard & Poor's 100) is a notable example of an index option with American-style exercise. Be sure to check the option exchange web site for the specifications of exercise for the options you are trading—don't be surprised!

When you have bought or sold stock option vertical spreads, early exercise of one or more of the options in your spreads is always a possibility, but actually only occurs under very specific circumstances. The owner of an equity option has the right to buy or sell 100 shares of the underlying stock anytime before expiration. If you are long the option (i.e., you originally bought it), you may or may not choose to exercise the option you own; it is entirely your choice. If you are short the option (i.e., you originally sold the option), it may be exercised against you at any time. Typically, you will receive an email from your broker after the market closes, notifying you of the exercise. You may be exercised for only a portion of your option position, for example, only two of your ten contracts. If you were short call options, you will now see a short stock position in your account (i.e., you were obligated to sell the stock at the strike price). If you were short put options, the exercise forces you to buy stock at the strike price, resulting in a long stock position in your account.

Early exercise with vertical spreads is normally not anything to be concerned about. If we owned ten contracts of an IBM call spread and three of our short calls were exercised against us, we would then be short 300 shares of IBM (i.e., we sold 300 shares of IBM to satisfy the exercise). We could then ask our broker to exercise three of our long IBM calls and buy 300 shares of stock. Now the short position in IBM is eliminated, and we have the spread difference in our account (i.e., $3,000 if a $10 spread) and seven remaining call spreads.

In practice, it is rare that your short option positions will be exercised against you before expiration. But, as noted earlier, your long option position protects you against this exercise. In general, put options are rarely exercised unless there is less than $0.10 of time value left in the option. The same is true of call options with one major exception: calls are often exercised just before a stock goes ex-dividend; for example, if the call has $0.10 of time value remaining, but the dividend is $0.50 per share, it will be advantageous to the option owner to exercise the option and hold the stock through the ex-dividend date to collect the dividend payment. Sometimes an option will be exercised against you in a situation where it makes no sense whatsoever and is probably a mistake or due to the inexperience of the person on the other side of the trade.

The following hypothetical situation illustrates the pros and cons of early exercise. On September 15, 2009, Bob bought ten contracts of the Oct Apple Computer (AAPL) $170/$175 call spread for $3,050 (AAPL was trading at $175.16). At the same time, Jim bought the ten contracts of the Oct AAPL $175 calls Bob sold for $6,100. About two weeks later, AAPL is trading at $185.32 and Bob could sell his spread for $4,100, representing a gain of $1,050. But if he waits until expiration and AAPL is still trading above $175, his spread will be worth $5,000. At the same time, Jim is very pleased with his investment; his $175 calls are worth $11,750. Jim has two choices:

1. Exercise his calls to buy 1,000 shares of AAPL at $175 for $175,000, and then sell those shares in the market for $185,320; after subtracting the $6,100 of the original purchase, Jim nets a $4,220 profit.
2. Sell the calls for $11,750 for a net $5,650 profit.

When Jim sells the calls, he is receiving compensation for the remaining time value in the options, whereas when he exercised the calls, the time value was lost. The Oct $175 call was selling for $11.75 and had $10.32 of intrinsic value (185.32 − 175). If Jim had exercised the call, he would have realized the $10.32 of intrinsic value but would have lost the $1.43 or $1,430 of time value.

This illustrates why options are usually not exercised early if any time value is remaining. If you are short call options that have gone in-the-money (ITM), then watch the remaining time value and be aware of any possible upcoming dividend payments for stockholders.

The situation is analogous for holding short put options, only without the exception for dividend payments. Therefore, if you are short put options that have moved ITM, watch the remaining time value in your short puts. When the time value has decayed sufficiently, early exercise becomes more likely. However, with vertical spreads, you always have a long option that protects you in the event of early exercise.

EXPIRATION AND EXERCISE

Upon expiration, your broker will automatically exercise any expiring options in your account that are $0.01 or more ITM in accordance with Options Clearing Corporation regulations. If expiration is approaching and the stock price is near your strike price, and you do not want to hold either the long or short stock position that will result from the exercise of your long option, sell the option before the market closes on the Friday of expiration week. If you are holding a European-style index option position and wish to close it before expiration, be sure to complete those orders before the market closes on Thursday before expiration. If you wish to exercise any of your long equity options, you must issue an order to your broker before the market closes on the Friday of expiration week. It is generally good practice to close option positions before expiration to avoid unpleasant surprises.

If you are holding a vertical spread position going into expiration, there are several different situations possible. If both of the options are fully in-the-money, your broker will automatically exercise both of the long and short options and credit your account with the spread amount less commissions. However, if the stock price closes on expiration Friday within the spread, the situation is a little tricky, and the results may surprise you.

Consider the situation where we are holding ten contracts of a bull call spread at the strike prices $100 and $110, and the stock closes at $109 on expiration Friday. The short $110 calls will expire worthless and the broker will exercise the $100 calls on your behalf, resulting in 1,000 shares of stock in your account the following Monday (and perhaps a call from your broker if your account does not have sufficient cash to buy the stock). If you do not want to purchase the stock, you should close the spread before the market closes on the Friday of expiration week.

Credit spreads can also result in surprises at expiration. For example, if I have sold ten contracts of the $170/$180 bull put spread and the underlying stock closes on the Friday of expiration week at $178, my short $180 put options will be exercised against me, resulting in my purchase of 1,000 shares of the stock. The long put option does not protect me because it expired worthless. If you did not have sufficient capital in the account to purchase the stock, you would have to either deposit funds in the account on Monday or sell the stock, perhaps at a loss. In some cases, your broker may close the spread Friday afternoon to limit the firm's exposure.

In general, if the stock price closes on expiration Friday within the strike prices of my vertical spread, it will result in either a long stock position or a short stock position in my account the following Monday. Unless you are willing to hold that stock position, it is usually best to close the spread on Friday. Many traders adopt a general rule of closing all option positions the week before expiration to avoid the surprises that are all too common the week of expiration.

MARGIN REQUIREMENTS

When opening a stock trading account, one always has the option of establishing a cash account or a margin account. If you have a margin account, you have the ability to buy more shares of a stock by borrowing additional funds from the brokerage firm. This is known as *buying on margin* and can lead to *margin calls* if the stock price declines. The margin call will require the deposit of additional funds or the sale of the stock position. Each month's statement will include interest charged by the broker for the margin.

We also speak of margin requirements in options trading accounts, but the concept is completely different; no borrowing is involved. When you establish an options position in your account, the broker determines the worst-case scenario and sets aside a *margin requirement* in your account and does not allow you to establish any new positions with those funds. The money is still in your account and earns interest, but can be thought of as being placed in escrow. This insures the broker in the event the position takes its maximum potential loss. The broker wants to be sure you can't lose more money than on deposit in the account because the brokerage would be exposed to that loss if you catch the plane to Acapulco.

For example, I establish an $80/$90 bull put spread for a $2,000 credit on ten contracts. The cash balance in my account increases by $2,000, but the broker sets aside $10,000 as a margin requirement, including the $2,000 credit. In the worst-case scenario, the maximum loss for that ten-contract spread would be $10,000, hence the margin requirement of $10,000. I will be unable to use this $10,000 for any other trades until this credit spread is closed.

Portfolio margin is a relatively new concept in options brokerage accounts. It calculates the margin requirement with a probability-based assessment of the risk of the trade, often resulting in much smaller margin requirements. Not all brokerages offer portfolio margin and the eligibility rules differ widely. Inquire with your broker to see if they offer portfolio margin and to determine the brokerage's requirements.

APPLICATION OF PROBABILITY CALCULATIONS

In Chapter 2, we discussed the use of probability distributions and distinguished the high-probability trade from the low-probability trade. We can use those same calculations to compare several vertical spreads under consideration for a trade. In Table 4.3, we are considering several possible debit call spreads that are deep ITM with a high probability of success. Each spread is set up for ten contracts.

In each case, we have calculated the probability of the stock price's closing above the spread at expiration. We might have been tempted to simply look at how far ITM our spread would be as an indication of how safe the trade was; for example, GOOG could drop $40, and that spread would still be profitable. But the NKE spread has a similar probability of

TABLE 4.3 Probability of Success for Selected Call Debit Spreads

Stock	Price ($)	Spread	Debit ($)	Max Profit ($)	Return (%)	Probability (%)	ITM ($)
TIVO	9	2.5/7.5	4,720	280	6	75	1.5
GOOG	530	480/490	9,100	900	10	90	40
IBM	122	105/115	9,730	270	3	88	7
NKE	64	55/60	4,900	100	2	88	4
POT	99	80/90	9,100	900	10	81	9
AAPL	192	165/175	9,200	800	9	87	17

TABLE 4.4 Risk-Adjusted Returns for Selected Debit Spreads

Stock	Price ($)	Spread	Max Profit ($)	Return (%)	Probability (%)	Risk-Adjusted Return (%)
TIVO	9	2.5/7.5	280	6	75	4.5
GOOG	530	480/490	900	10	90	9
IBM	122	105/115	270	3	88	2.6
NKE	64	55/60	100	2	88	1.8
POT	99	80/90	900	10	81	8
AAPL	192	165/175	800	9	87	8

success and yet is only $4 ITM. The probability calculation has enabled a much better comparison of the true risk of these trades.

We can take it one step further by computing the risk-adjusted returns in Table 4.4.

In this example, the trader was searching for a high-probability trade; computing the probabilities of success and then the risk-adjusted returns allowed him to narrow consideration to a smaller number of candidates. In this example, the trader might narrow his focus to GOOG, POT, and AAPL; all three have a probability of success of about 80% to 90% and a risk-adjusted return of 8% to 9%.

RISK/REWARD AND PROBABILITY OF SUCCESS

Applying our probability calculations to vertical spreads reinforces the conclusions we drew in Chapter 2 about high- and low-probability trades. Consider the data in the Table 4.5 for the hypothetical stock XYZ, trading at $109. We buy three call spreads: one is ITM, one is at-the-money (ATM), and one is out-of-the-money (OTM).

TABLE 4.5 Probability Characteristics of Vertical Spreads

Bull Call Spreads	Maximum Return	Risk/ Reward	Probability of Break-even
OTM $110/$120	365%	0.27	30%
ATM $100/$110	38%	2.6	58%
ITM $95/$105	11%	9.0	74%

The ITM vertical spread has the highest probability of breaking even, but it also has the lowest maximum return at 11%. This is the classic high-probability trade we discussed at length in Chapter 2. The high probability of success is accompanied by a high risk/reward ratio; that is, while we have a 74% probability of at least breaking even, we have a small probability of losing our entire investment in the trade.

The OTM vertical spread represents the opposite extreme, the low-probability trade. It boasts the highest potential return, but also has the lowest probability of breaking even. The OTM spread has a low risk/reward ratio, meaning the potential return is huge but the probabilities are against our achieving that return.

Each of these spreads is feasible for the trader who is bullish on XYZ. But it is crucial to understand the trade-offs in risk and reward as well as the probabilities of success for these positions.

EXERCISES

1. In general terms, how do I establish an options spread?
2. Where do vertical spreads get their name?
3. If I am bullish on IBM at today's price, what two different types of vertical spreads could I establish? Compute the maximum profit, maximum loss, and break-even of each spread.
4. What are the margin requirements for the two spreads in question 3?
5. Which of the two spreads in question 3 is the better choice? Why?
6. If I were bullish on IBM at $118, what would be an example of an aggressive bullish spread versus a conservative bullish spread?
7. I buy a GOOG $490/$500 call spread for $450 just a few days before the earnings announcement and IV is at record high levels. IV collapses after the announcement and two weeks later both options expire ITM. What profit, if any, did I make? What effect did the change in IV have on my position?
8. I was bearish on IBM when it was trading at $113, and I sold the $115/$110 call spread. Several weeks later, IBM is trading for $98 and I want to close the position. What orders would you place to close the spread?
9. The IBM position in question 8 can be closed with one order or two separate orders. What are the pros and cons of the two approaches?
10. My account balance is $25,200. I sell 20 GOOG $510/$520 call spreads for $534/contract. What is my account balance after placing this trade? How much margin will be required?

11. As I approach expiration Friday with the GOOG spread above, GOOG is trading at $510. What choices do you have? What would you recommend?

12. I own 15 IBM $100/$110 call spreads. We are three days from expiration and IBM is trading at $123. Is early exercise of the short $110 calls likely? What would you do?

PART 2

Options Strategies for Income Generation

CHAPTER 5

Using Options to Boost Income in a Stock Portfolio

W e can broadly divide options trading strategies into two very distinct camps:

- Directional or speculative strategies
- Nondirectional or delta-neutral strategies

The two strategies we will discuss in this chapter, covered calls and selling naked puts, are both a bit of a hybrid between directional and nondirectional strategies. The covered call strategy can be used to boost the income from your stock holdings while the market is slightly bullish or trading sideways. But if your opinion of the market's future direction is bearish, the covered call is not the appropriate strategy.

We can use the selling naked puts strategy to either generate income or build a stock position at a discount. But selling naked puts depends on a bullish market trend or, at a minimum, a sideways trend.

Chapters 6, 7, and 8 will concentrate on nondirectional or delta-neutral options trading strategies. Some will argue that the delta-neutral strategy also requires a market prediction, namely, a prediction of a sideways market. But I maintain that a delta-neutral options strategy does not require the trader to predict a sideways market trend *if* he knows how to adjust his position for a strongly trending market. Then the trader can play the delta-neutral strategy every month. He will profit in the months where the market either trades sideways or trends slowly; he will take small losses or break even when the market trends strongly against his positions. The delta-neutral trader is profitable longer term only when applying robust risk management techniques.

This chapter will focus on using options within your long-term stock portfolio account to generate extra income in slower periods of the market.

THE CLASSIC COVERED CALL STRATEGY

Let's assume I have 500 shares of IBM in my stock portfolio. IBM is trading at $123, and the market appears to be in a consolidating, sideways trend. I decide to sell five contracts of the March $125 calls for $2.50. This brings $1,250 into my account, or about 2% of my IBM holdings.

Now, fast-forward to March expiration. If IBM is trading unchanged at $123, those $125 calls will expire worthless and I will have gained $1,250 while the market was just treading water. If IBM surprises me and spurts up to $130, then the option I sold will be exercised, requiring me to sell my 500 shares of IBM for $125 per share. My gain will be $2,250, or 3.7% based on my original position of IBM stock at $123 per share ($1,000 on the stock price appreciation plus the $1,250 from selling the call). This scenario illustrates the derivation of the *covered call* name. My short option has been exercised against me, requiring me to sell 500 shares of IBM stock at $125 per share. I would incur a large loss if I had to buy IBM at the market price of $130 and turn around and sell it for $125. But I already own the IBM shares, so I am "covered."

Covered calls are also known as *buy-writes* because you buy the stock and then effectively "write" or create a call option in the process of selling the call.

In the preceding scenario, where IBM has traded up to $130, I would be up $3,500, or 5.7%, if I had just held the stock and not sold a call. So selling the call has limited my upside profit potential. In return, I have locked in a limited income stream in the event IBM trades sideways or slightly upward to just under $125.

However, if IBM drops to $120, the March $125 calls will expire worthless, and I will be down $250 (I lost $1,500 on the stock but brought in $1,250 by selling the call). One of the advantages of the covered call is that it limits your downside risk somewhat, but not entirely. You still have most of the downside risk of the stock ownership position.

In summary, the covered call brings in additional income if the stock trades sideways and limits a small portion of the downside risk, but does this at the cost of limiting our upside profit potential. With a covered call, you are purposely giving up the "home run" in return for a more predictable, steady income stream.

STRATEGIC CONSIDERATIONS

Your prediction of the future price move for this stock is foundational to several decisions concerning the configuration of the covered call. If I am bearish on this stock, I might sell the first in-the-money (ITM) call option to bring in a larger premium and better limit my downside loss. Of course, at some point, I am probably better advised to simply sell my stock. If my prediction were for a sideways price move, I would sell the option either at-the-money (ATM) or just out-of-the-money (OTM). I might move one more strike OTM if I am slightly bullish, but now I am reaching the limits of the covered call strategy; if I am bullish on this stock, I should just hold the stock and not sell any calls.

Some traders buy stock specifically for the covered call strategy and wish to maximize their monthly income by selling the ATM call. In these cases, high-priced stocks are a disadvantage due to the large investment of capital necessary for the trade.

High levels of implied volatility (IV) will increase the potential returns for the covered call due to the elevated prices of the call options. However, remember why IV is high for that stock—the market is anticipating some upcoming event. It may be an earnings announcement, a Food and Drug Administration (FDA) announcement of the conclusion of a clinical trial, an expected legal decision, or something similar. In other words, high IV means higher risk of a large price move up or down. Whenever the potential returns for a covered call trade appear exceptionally attractive, be sure you understand why those options are priced that high.

The covered call strategy is fundamentally a neutral to bullish strategy. If the market is trending downward, the covered call is probably not the optimal strategy. However, if you need to hold your stock position for some other reason, selling ATM or slightly ITM calls will help limit your losses while the market drops.

THE NOTORIOUS SELLING NAKED PUTS STRATEGY

Selling naked puts is one of the more notorious options trading strategies. Horror stories abound of traders completely wiping out their accounts when they were short large numbers of puts as the market crashed. However, these disastrous anecdotes underscore the need for proper risk management as much as anything. We will cover risk management in detail in a few pages. Let's focus on the selling naked puts strategy for a moment.

When we sell puts on a stock, we are "naked" because we are not covered in the event the short put is exercised. For example, assume we sell five contracts of the Google (GOOG) May $580 puts for $32.80 while GOOG is trading at $563. That brings $16,400 into our account. If GOOG is trading above $580 at May expiration, the puts expire worthless and we keep the $16,400 as our profit. That's attractive. However, if GOOG closes unchanged at expiration at $563, those puts will be exercised, forcing us to buy 500 shares of GOOG at $580 per share, or $290,000. If we have the cash in our account to accept that exercise, then that may be acceptable, because our cost for those shares is $547.20 ($580 − $32.80), so I could turn around and sell those shares on Monday for a tidy profit. But if I have only $100,000 in my account and my broker calls on the Monday after expiration and wants to know when I am bringing the other $190,000 into the office, I may have a problem. Or worse, if GOOG opens up Monday at $500, I have a big problem.

Some traders make it a practice to sell far OTM options month after month and just collect their profits each month as the options expire worthless. And since OTM options are priced very inexpensively, those traders will be selling large numbers of contracts to collect a meaningful potential profit. But if I am short a large number of puts and the market crashes, I can lose huge amounts of money overnight. Hence, we have the notorious reputation of selling naked puts. This underscores the need for robust risk management when selling naked puts, which will be addressed later in this chapter.

SELLING NAKED PUTS FOR INCOME

The strategy of selling naked puts may be used to generate income or as a strategy for accumulating a stock position at a discount to the current market price.

This strategy, like covered calls, presumes a bullish market for its success. In the example of the preceding section, we sold the GOOG $580 puts while GOOG was trading at $563. If GOOG trades upward and closes at expiration above $580, then the option we sold expires worthless, and we keep the income from that option sale as our profit. The policies of options brokers vary, but a margin requirement of 25% to 30% is typical for selling naked puts in a cash account. Selling naked puts in an individual retirement account (IRA) is usually required to be fully cash secured; that is, all of the cash necessary to buy the stock should the put be exercised is held in the account and cannot be used for other trades.

Figure 5.1 shows the risk/reward graph for the sale of the GOOG $580 puts in our example. Notice that our downside risk is huge and

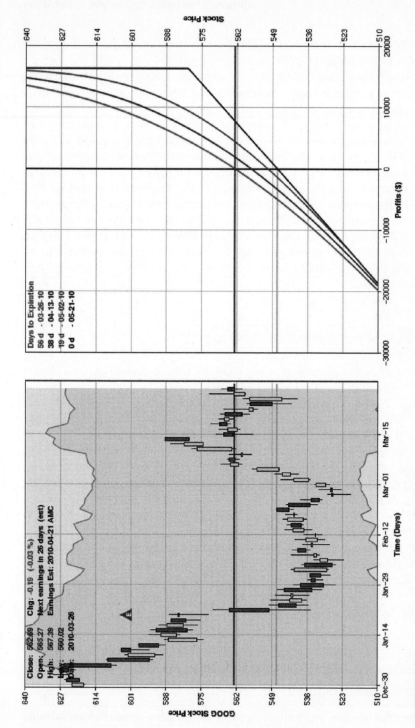

FIGURE 5.1 GOOG Naked Put Risk/Reward Graph

Source: Screenshots provided courtesy of Optionetics Platinum © 2010. All rights reserved, etc.

virtually unlimited. But I have plotted the risk/reward graph for a covered call on GOOG in Figure 5.2.

It is often surprising for many people to see that the risk/reward curves for these two trading strategies are identical. Both have a limited potential profit and virtually unlimited downside risk.

Returning to our GOOG example, imagine if we were selling this put in our retirement account. We would have a margin requirement of $273,600 ($290,000 − $16,400), and thus our maximum profit would be 6%. If this trade were in a cash account and our broker charges a 25% margin requirement, then the $16,400 return would be on $72,500 of capital at risk, or 23%.

The risk/reward characteristics of the covered call and selling naked put strategies are identical. The returns for a fully cash-secured naked put trade will be very similar to those of the covered call. The reduced margin requirements for the naked put when held in a cash account makes it more attractive. But one should never forget the downside risk present in both of these trades.

BUYING STOCKS AT A DISCOUNT

Many famous stock investors have used the sale of naked puts as a means of accumulating large positions of stock over time at favorable prices. Working from our example above with Google, let's assume you have decided that you want Google to be one of your core stock holdings and have targeted 400 shares as the appropriate portion in your portfolio.

One approach you might take would be to simply buy 400 shares at $563 per share for a total investment of $225,200. Another approach would be to sell four contracts of the $580 puts at $32.80. If Google closes at $563 on expiration, the puts will be exercised and you will purchase 400 shares at $580 per share. But your net cost basis is $547.20. You purchased Google on sale for a 3% or $16 per share discount.

If you were managing a large fund and accumulating shares of Google, you might sell ten contracts each month. Some months, the puts might expire worthless; other months, you would buy the shares at discount. Over time, you would accumulate the desired position at a lower cost than simply purchasing the stock.

COMBINING THE COVERED CALL WITH SELLING NAKED PUTS

A powerful income generation strategy is to combine selling naked puts with covered calls month after month. You are now selling option premium

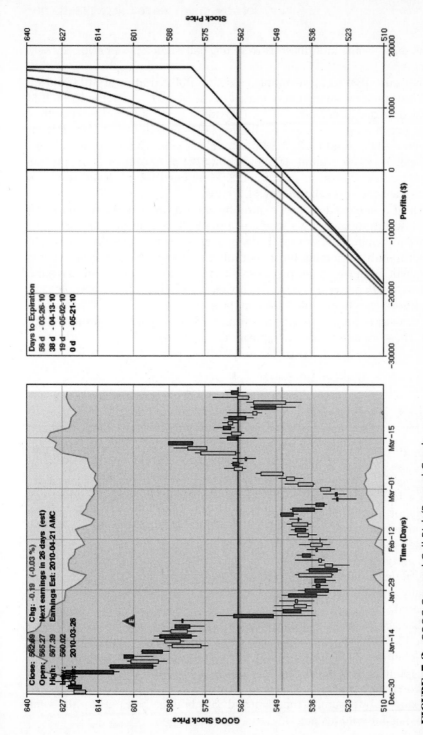

FIGURE 5.2 GOOG Covered Call Risk/Reward Graph

Source: Screenshots provided courtesy of Optionetics Platinum © 2010. All rights reserved, etc.

for income—some months you are selling calls; some months you are selling puts.

Let's use IBM as our example. Assume IBM is trading at $123, and we start our trade by selling one contract of the Mar $125 puts for $4.45. IBM closes on expiration Friday at $124.25 and the put is exercised, resulting in our purchasing 100 shares of IBM for $125 per share or $12,500. But we collected $445, or about 3.5% of our purchase price. Now we sell the Apr $125 call for $3.30. Assume IBM closes at $124 at April expiration; the call will expire worthless, so we earned 2.6% on our IBM stock position, and we turn around and sell the May $125 calls.

Or, if IBM closed at April expiration at $126, we would have our stock purchased from us and we would sell the $125 puts in May and start the cycle over again. This strategy is deceptively powerful. One can earn 2% to 4% per month; projecting these monthly returns to 24% to 48% per year is unrealistic because our stop losses will be triggered on occasion. But earning 18% to 20% per year is a realistic expectation. Over time, we would shift the strike prices being sold based on the stock price movement. But, again, this strategy assumes we have a neutral to slightly bullish environment for IBM. These strategies are not appropriate for bear markets.

EARLY EXERCISE

When you are selling naked puts for income and you do not want to purchase the stock, it is important to know when you may be at risk for an early exercise of the put option. Options are rarely exercised when more than a few cents of time value remain in the option's price. When you have short puts in your account that are ITM, as they often are when you sell naked puts, watch the time value in the puts carefully. As long as the put has more than $0.10 of time value remaining, you are probably safe from early exercise. But that is never a certainty, so it is wise to always have the cash necessary to cover the exercise of your short puts. Occasionally, options are exercised by mistake or by a novice, so one must be prepared.

Let's consider an example to illustrate the principles involved. On October 15, 2009, Apple Computer (AAPL) was trading at $190.56. Joe sells the November $200 put for $14.17. Two other traders, Sam and Sally, both own 100 shares of AAPL, and each buys a Nov $200 put to protect their position from a pullback. This is summarized in Table 5.1. I have simplified the example by assuming that Sam and Sally bought their puts for the same price that Joe sold his put.

TABLE 5.1 Early Exercise Example

Date	AAPL	Nov $200 Put	Remaining Time Value	Joe	Sam	Sally
10/15/09	$190.56	$14.17	$4.70	Sells put for $1,417	Owns 100 shares AAPL; Buys put for $1,417	Owns 100 shares AAPL; Buys put for $1,417
10/28/09	$192.40	$10.80	$3.20	Buys 100 shares at $200; net cost = $185.83	Exercises put to sell shares; net income = $18,583	Sells put and shares; net income = $18,903
11/16/09	$188.00	$12.05	$0.05	Buys 100 shares at $200; net cost = $185.83	Exercises put to sell shares; net income = $18,583	Sells put and shares; net income = $18,588

On October 28, AAPL has traded up to $192.40 and the Nov $200 put is now trading for $10.80. Sam decides to close his position by exercising his put to sell his shares of AAPL for $200 per share and realizes $18,583 ($20,000 − $1,417). Sally has also decided to close her position, but she sells her stock at the market price and sells her put, resulting in a net $18,903, or $320 better than Sam's ending cash position. Sally gained the $3.20 of time value left in the put by selling it rather than exercising the put option. However, as we near expiration and the time value is now only a nickel, the difference in Sam's and Sally's positions is very small.

This example also demonstrates the power of selling naked puts to establish a stock position. Joe could have bought his Apple Computer stock for $190.56 on October 15 when he sold the put; instead, he paid a net cost of $185.83, a savings of $4.73 per share or 2.5%.

If you have short puts in your account that are ITM and you do not wish to buy the underlying stock, monitor the remaining time value in those puts and close the position before the remaining time value reaches $0.10 or less.

RISK MANAGEMENT

Risk management is critical for any investment or trading activity. As mentioned earlier, the downside risk for covered calls and selling naked puts is substantial. We have limited our upside profit potential but have done very little to limit our downside risk. Therefore, risk management is especially critical for these strategies. It is ironic that many consider covered calls to be a conservative strategy, and thus risk management doesn't receive much attention. It is also ironic that many retail traders view selling naked puts as very risky and yet the risk/reward graphs for the covered call and selling naked puts are identical, as we saw in Figures 5.1 and 5.2.

Long-term stock positions should always be protected by an automated trailing stop-loss order placed with the broker. If a stock portfolio is using covered calls on an occasional basis to augment portfolio income during lulls in the market, then the stop-loss orders will have to be modified to buy back the calls that were sold and then sell the stock.

If one is buying stocks specifically for use with a covered call strategy for income generation, then the stop-loss order is more straightforward. Immediately after establishing the covered call position, enter a stop-loss order to buy back the calls and sell the stock if the stock price drops below your trigger price. Determining the trigger price is a personal choice based on risk tolerance and trading style. If you place it too close to the current stock price, many trades will be stopped out prematurely. But if you place it farther down in price, you incur the risk of larger losses. When I am using the covered call with more volatile stocks to generate higher levels of income, I generally place my stop just below the break-even price for the covered call trade.

One may be selling naked puts against high-volatility stocks for income generation or using the sale of naked puts to build a stock position at favorable prices. In either case, risk management is crucial. It is recommended that you set your stop-loss order to trigger if the stock price drops below the break-even price for the position (i.e., the strike price of the put sold minus the premium received).

When selling puts for income, one should also monitor the time value remaining in the option if it is ITM. Early exercise isn't an issue for the stock accumulation strategy, but it would, at a minimum, be an inconvenience in an income generation strategy.

Consider the nature of the stock when selling puts against it; this is a crucial aspect of the risk inherent in this strategy. Holding short puts on a blue-chip stock is far different from the short put position on a biotechnology stock. An unexpected FDA announcement could erase much of the biotechnology stock's price overnight. Your stop-loss order may be helpful, but it is far from a perfect hedge against that downside risk.

THE ACHILLES' HEEL OF DIRECTIONAL STRATEGIES

The covered call and selling naked puts strategies are only suitable for neutral to bullish markets. In fact, the covered call should not be used in strong bullish markets because you are giving up too much upside potential. One of the most basic stock investment rules is to "trade with the trend." We need to have reasonable expectations of at least a neutral market, if not slightly bullish, for these strategies to be feasible. Trying to pick winning stocks in the midst of a bear market is very difficult. Selling calls against my stock provides only minimal downside protection. So the trader's ability to judge the market trend is crucial to selling calls or puts in these strategies.

That brings us to a crucial question. Can you predict the trend? This is the critical success factor with directional options strategies. For optimal success, you need to be trading with the trend. In the following chapters, we will discuss nondirectional or delta-neutral options trading strategies. Freeing oneself from the need to predict the market's direction is very powerful. That is the significant advantage of delta-neutral trading strategies.

EXERCISES

1. Why is the covered call "covered" and a naked put position "uncovered" or "naked"?

2. How could you use the selling naked puts strategy?

3. True or false: the covered call strategy is more conservative than the selling naked puts strategy. Why or why not?

4. Compare and contrast the expected returns for the covered call strategy vs. the selling naked puts strategy.

5. Assume the naked puts margin requirement for your broker is 25% for the following questions.

   a. Assume AAPL is trading at $182. If my expectation for AAPL were slightly bullish, which put would you sell? If we sold the $185 put for $8.30, what is the maximum return on ten contracts? Under what circumstances will we achieve that return?

   b. If the preceding trade were placed in my IRA, what would the maximum return be?

6. Assume I sold ten contracts of the Sept $170 AAPL put for $5.60 a couple of weeks ago. As I approach September expiration, AAPL is trading at $182 and the Sept $170 put is trading at $0.05 × $0.07. What should I do and why?

7. I have an account with a $50,000 balance. Earlier, I sold five contracts of the Sept $480 puts for GOOG. As we near expiration, GOOG is trading at $488. What should I do and why?

8. I sold one contract of the Sept $180 puts for AAPL. On expiration Friday, AAPL closes at $188. What will happen? If AAPL had closed at $179, what would have happened?

9. What safeguards should I employ when selling naked puts?

10. Develop covered call scenarios for RIMM (trading at $82) and selling the $85 call at $5.50, and for GOOG (trading at $488) and selling the $490 call at $15.80. Assume you have a $50,000 account, and all positions are called away at expiration.

    a. Work out the potential returns for investing all of your account in a covered call trade for (1) RIMM and (2) GOOG.

    b. Why are the results so different?

CHAPTER 6

Calendar and Double Calendar Spreads

C alendar spreads are created by buying an option in a future expiration month and selling an option at the same strike price in the current or front expiration month. Calendar spreads are also known as *time spreads* or *horizontal spreads*. The horizontal spread terminology derives from the original boards in the exchange used to post option prices. When we create the calendar spread, we are buying and selling options in the same row (same strike price) but in different columns (different expiration months), hence the horizontal spread.

As we saw earlier, one of the factors determining an option's price is the remaining time before the option expires. As the price drops due to less time remaining to expiration, we refer to this phenomenon as *time decay*. But that time decay is not a linear function; it accelerates as the date of expiration approaches. The profitability of the calendar spread is built on the differential in time decay between the front-month option and the longer-term option. We have sold the front-month option, and it is decaying in price faster than the longer-term option that we own.

We will create a calendar spread with Apple Computer (AAPL) to illustrate the basic characteristics of this spread. On February 12, 2010, AAPL was trading at $200, and we created a $200 Mar/Apr call calendar spread for a debit of $340. The risk/reward graph is illustrated in Figure 6.1.

You can immediately see why the calendar spread is attractive with its broad break-even range from $191 to $211. This trade has a potential profit of 20% or more over a large portion of that break-even range. This AAPL calendar was created with call options, but one may also create a put calendar as in Figure 6.2.

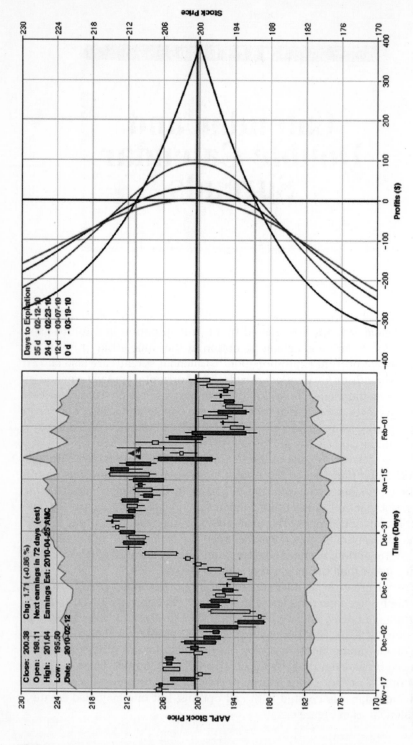

FIGURE 6.1 AAPL Mar/APR $200 Call Calendar Spread

Source: Screenshots provided courtesy of Optionetics Platinum © 2010. All rights reserved, etc.

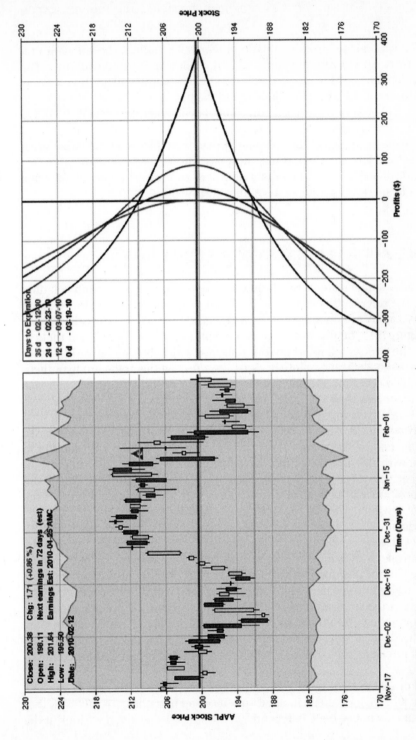

FIGURE 6.2 AAPL Mar/Apr $200 Put Calendar Spread
Source: Screenshots provided courtesy of Optionetics Platinum © 2010. All rights reserved, etc.

65

As you can see from comparing Figures 6.1 and 6.2, the calendar created from calls is virtually identical to the calendar created with puts. The put calendar would require a debit of $333 to establish and has break-evens at $191 and $210. The call calendar and the put calendar at the same strike prices will be very close to the same initial debit and have virtually identical risk/reward graphs.

These examples of the calendar spread were placed at the strike price nearest the current stock price; these are known as *at-the-money (ATM) calendars* and are used in situations where you expect the stock or index to trade sideways within a reasonably narrow range.

VEGA RISK AND CALENDAR SPREADS

Calendar spreads are particularly sensitive to changes in implied volatility (IV). We refer to this as *vega risk*. As an example, let's assume we spent $1,700 to buy five contracts of the AAPL Mar/Apr $200 call calendar spread of Figure 6.1. The position Greeks are delta = $3, vega = $42, and theta = $11. The Greeks tell us where our risks are with this trade. If AAPL trades up by $5 to $205, and all other variables affecting this trade are hypothetically held constant, the delta of $3 tells us our position value will increase by $15, or less than 1%. Thus, we call this a *delta-neutral trade*—the position is relatively insensitive to the underlying stock's price movement.

Now consider the passage of time, or what we often call *theta decay* or *time decay*. The theta value of $11 tells us the position will gain $11 in value with the passage of one day; again, this is a relatively insignificant number. However, as this trade progresses, theta will grow in value, and the position will benefit more and more with the passage of time. Time decay is what drives the profitability of the calendar spread.

However, our vega value for this position is $42. An increase of only 2% in IV will increase the value of our position by $84, or about 5%. Conversely, a decrease of 2% in implied volatility will cause our position to lose 5% of its value. So our position has more sensitivity to changes in IV than anything else; we refer to calendar spreads as positions with *high vega risk*. When we are considering candidates for a calendar spread, it is critical that we compare the current level of IV with this stock's history of IV. Decreasing IV while in a calendar spread will destroy the trade's profitability even if the stock price has stayed exactly where we predicted for the trade's optimum outcome.

For example, if we are considering an ATM calendar spread on XYZ stock and we look up its implied volatility and find it is currently 35%, that may or may not be high. It depends on the stock. However, if we look at the history of IV for this stock and see that it has oscillated over the past year between 25% and 110%, we might feel more confident about this trade. It is more likely that the IV for XYZ will trade upward rather than downward, based on its historical pattern of movement.

A common pattern of IV movement for many stocks is to peak just before the quarterly earnings announcement and then immediately collapse to historically low values. In Google's early years after its initial public offering (IPO), IV would commonly run up to well over 100% just before its earnings announcement, drop down to about 25%, and then slowly build back to high values before the next earnings announcement. If a company is expecting a significant news event, like a Food and Drug Administration (FDA) announcement for a biotechnology company, we will see IV peak just before that announcement.

A critical success factor for trading calendar and double calendar spreads is to initiate the trade with the underlying stock or index at historically low values of implied volatility.

VOLATILITY SKEWS

Thus far, we have presumed that IV changes for a stock occur uniformly across the options chain, but that isn't always true in the real world. *Volatility skews* refer to situations where the IV of the front-month option that we sold is different from the IV of the option that we own in a later month.

A positive volatility skew develops when the IV of the front month is higher than the later months. Conversely, a calendar spread with a negative IV skew has long options in the later month with higher IV than the options sold in the front month. Recall what we learned about option pricing in Chapter 3: higher IV means higher option prices. Thus, we would prefer a positive volatility skew where we are selling the more expensive option and buying the less expensive option because our profitability is based on the more rapid time decay of the option we sold.

Higher IV develops because the market expects a big move on the stock price, either up or down—it is not a directional prediction. If that higher IV is in the front month so we have a positive volatility skew, then the event causing the market's anticipation must be expected in the front month. Similarly, in the case of a negative volatility skew, the market is expecting the catalyst for the big stock price move to occur in the later month.

An excellent example of this phenomenon is illustrated in Figures 6.3 and 6.4. Both of these hypothetical trades were created on August 25, 2009, with Google (GOOG) trading at $471. Figure 6.3 shows the risk/reward

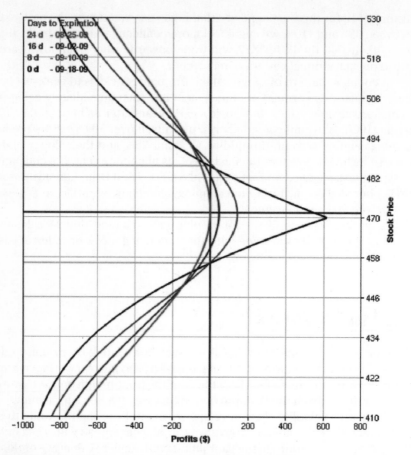

FIGURE 6.3 GOOG Sept/Oct $470 Call Calendar Spread
Source: Screenshots provided courtesy of Optionetics Platinum © 2010. All rights reserved, etc.

graph for the Sept/Oct $470 call calendar with a debit of $1,000, a maximum profit of 62%, and a break-even range of $456 to $485.

On the same date, we could have placed the Oct/Dec $470 call calendar for a debit of $880, a maximum profit of 159% and a break-even range of $436 to $512 (Figure 6.4).

The break-even range has more than doubled from $29 to $76, and the profitability has also more than doubled from 62% to 159%. Why is there such a dramatic difference in these calendar spreads? The answer lies within the volatility skew. The Sept/Oct $470 call calendar of Figure 6.3 has a negative volatility skew of nearly 6 points (some authors cite skews as a percentage difference in the two values of IV; I simply cite the difference in percentage points, i.e., $31.0 - 25.1 = 5.9$). The October calls have a much

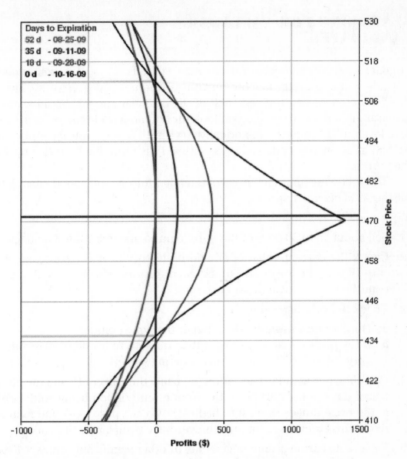

FIGURE 6.4 GOOG Oct/Dec $470 Call Calendar Spread
Source: Screenshots provided courtesy of Optionetics Platinum © 2010. All rights
reserved, etc.

higher IV than the September calls because the market was already looking
forward to Google's earnings announcement on October 15, so the October
calls were already starting to be bid up in price. But with the Oct/Dec $470
call calendar, we are selling the expensive options and we have a positive
IV skew of a little over two points. That leads to a much larger break-even
range and profit potential.

So we are left with two critical lessons for our calendar spreads:

1. Always ensure that the stock's IV is in the bottom quartile of its historical levels of IV before establishing the calendar spread.
2. Vega risk is the primary risk of the calendar spread; monitor IV changes
   closely while in the calendar spread trade.

SEARCHING FOR CALENDAR CANDIDATES

In general, good candidates for calendar spreads are stocks you expect to trade within a pretty narrow range over the next 30 days or so. However, as noted earlier, the vega risk of the calendar spread should always be paramount in your mind as you look for potential trade candidates. Current levels of IV must be historically low; in that way, you have put the probabilities on your side—in those cases, IV is more likely to rise rather than drop.

The following approach is recommended for finding a good candidate for the ATM calendar spread:

1. Sell about 25 to 30 days of time premium to maximize the time decay.

2. Check the current value of IV and its history over the past year. Be sure IV is in the lower 25% of its recent history. This is critical; if this condition isn't satisfied, stop here.

3. Check the volatility skew:

   a. Don't trade a negative skew larger than one point.
   b. If the positive skew is greater than three to four points, investigate very carefully. The market is expecting something.

4. Calculate one standard deviation (σ) using the current IV and the number of days to expiration for the front-month option being sold. Look at the price ranges (lowest to highest) over the past week and month. Avoid this stock if recent price moves have been larger than one σ.

5. Be sure no earnings announcements or other significant events are expected over the next 30 days.

6. Be sure you are selling at least $0.50 of time value in the front month; otherwise, trading commissions take too much of your profit.

7. Plot the risk/reward graph; be sure the break-even range will encompass any price movement you expect from this stock.

8. Estimate the likely return from the risk/reward graph if you close the trade one week before expiration. Be sure this is at least 30%. Disregard the maximum potential return at expiration; that return is unrealistic because we won't be taking the trade into expiration week, but it is also unlikely that the stock price will close at expiration right at the strike price of the calendar spread.

Lower-IV stocks, like the classic blue-chip stocks, will have a lower probability of making a large price move, but the option premiums tend to be small. However, high-volatility stocks have very rich option premiums, but the probability of a large move that triggers your stop-loss is also high. That is the trade-off the trader must manage when searching for candidates for the calendar spread.

ENTERING AND MANAGING THE TRADE

Enter your order for the calendar spread at the midpoint of the bid/ask spread. If the order isn't filled within one to two minutes, adjust the limit price upward by $0.05; continue this process until the order fills. Be patient; every nickel counts, especially when trading more conservative, low-IV stocks.

Write down the following in your trading journal:

- Set stop-loss prices (set at the break-even prices or slightly beyond).
- Set an overriding stop-loss of a 25% loss on the position.
- Set a minimum profit expectation based on the maximum gain expected one week before expiration. If the expected gain is 50%, set the minimum profit at 25%. When the position is up 25%, close half of the contracts and close the balance of the contracts on any pullbacks.
- Monitor IV of the individual legs of the trade; on any IV decrease greater than one to two percentage points, close the trade. If a negative IV skew develops, close the trade.
- On the Friday before expiration week, close the position or roll to the next month if the trade is a multiple-month calendar spread; for example, with an Oct/Jan calendar, as you near Oct expiration, you could roll to Nov (buy back Oct and sell Nov).

EARLY EXERCISE

We discussed the aspects of early exercise or assignment of our short option positions in vertical spreads in Chapter 4 and when selling naked puts in Chapter 5. Those principles apply to the short option positions within calendar spreads as well, but with some minor nuances. All stock options may be exercised on any business day prior to expiration. These are known as American-style options. European-style options can be exercised only at expiration. Most, but not all, broad index options are European style (e.g., Standard & Poor's 500 Index, Russell 2000 Index, Nasdaq 100 Index, and others). But the Standard & Poor's 100 (OEX) is a notable example of an index option with American-style exercise. Be sure to check the option exchange web site for the specifications of exercise for the options you are trading—don't be surprised!

When you have bought calendar spreads on the underlying stock, early exercise of the short front-month options is always a possibility, but this occurs only under very specific circumstances. In one sense, early exercise of the front-month option isn't a concern since the long option in the later month can be exercised to protect the assignment. However, we would lose a significant amount of time value with the exercise of that later-month option, so we wish to avoid that scenario.

Your short option positions are unlikely to be exercised against you before expiration unless two conditions are met:

1. The short option is in-the-money (ITM).

2. There is less than $0.10 of time value remaining in the option. As noted in Chapter 4, the exception to this would occur with short call options if a dividend has been declared with more value than the remaining time value of the option.

Monitor your calendar spread positions carefully when they are ITM and expiration is approaching. If the time value drops to $0.10 or less, either close or roll the position.

ADJUSTMENTS

Until you gain some experience with calendar spreads, simply close the spreads when the price trips your stop-loss price or the position stop-loss is exceeded. In fact, many experienced traders do not adjust the calendar spread; they just follow the stop-loss guidelines outlined above.

Use the break-even prices to trigger the adjustment. When the adjustment triggers, close half of your spreads and open new calendars at a strike price close to the current stock price. For example, if we opened ten contracts of a $120 call calendar on IBM when it was trading at $120, and IBM has now traded up to $130 and crossed our upper break-even price, we would close five contracts of the $120 call calendars and open five contracts at $130.

Don't adjust the calendar spread if you have less than 15 days left to expiration. However, if·you have a multiple-month calendar spread, you could buy back the current-month options and sell the following month. For example, if we have ten contracts of the IBM Oct/Jan $120 call calendar and IBM has traded up to $130 with only eight days left until October expiration, we could buy back ten contracts of the Oct $120 calls and sell ten contracts of the Nov $130 calls. Now you have diagonalized the trade (more in Chapter 7) and can continue to build profit in the position as IBM trades higher. If your assessment of IBM was more sideways to bearish at this point, you could buy back all ten of the Oct $120 calls and sell ten Nov $120 calls to create a new Nov/Jan $120 calendar spread. This is referred to as rolling the calendar out in time.

OUT-OF-THE-MONEY CALENDAR SPREADS

While the ATM calendar spread is a classic delta-neutral trade, one may place the calendar spread out-of-the-money (OTM) to speculate on a directional move. If I am bullish on a stock, I could place a call calendar spread above the current stock price. OTM calendars are usually inexpensive positions and will dramatically gain in value as the stock price trades upward.

If I am bearish on a stock, I could place a put calendar spread below the current stock price. As the stock price trades downward, the put calendar will increase in value.

OTM calendar spreads are speculative trades, and therefore are not the focus of this book. But they are the building blocks for the double calendar spread, a powerful delta-neutral income generation trade.

DOUBLE CALENDAR SPREADS

The *double calendar* spread is formed with an OTM call calendar above the stock price and an OTM put calendar down below the stock price. When used together, these speculative, directional trades form a delta-neutral, nondirectional trade. Let's continue with our Apple Computer example from earlier, where we placed a $200 call calendar ATM for $340 with a break-even range from $190 to $211. Figure 6.5 is the risk/reward graph for the AAPL Mar/Apr 190/210 double call calendar formed with two OTM calendar spreads: one $190 put calendar and one $210 call calendar.

The AAPL double calendar has increased the break-even range somewhat: $186 to $215. But the investment has increased to $605 and the profitability is disappointing. Note the dipping of the risk/reward curves in the middle. That is your clue to the negative volatility skew that is hurting this trade's profit potential. If AAPL trades between $195 and $205 and we hold this trade to about 12 days to expiration, we could expect a return of about 15%. This range of profitability is too narrow and the return is too small. The negative volatility skew is the culprit.

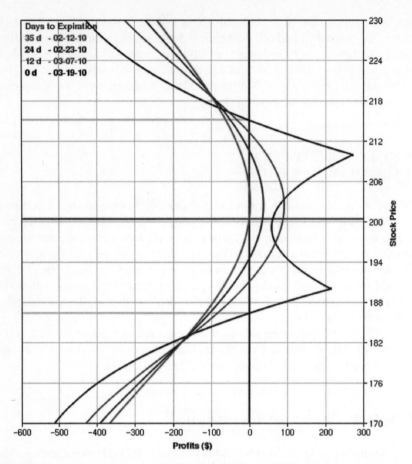

FIGURE 6.5   AAPL Mar/Apr 190/210 Double Call Calendar Spread
Source: Screenshots provided courtesy of Optionetics Platinum © 2010. All rights
reserved, etc.

If we move back in time to November 2, 2009, and place the AAPL
Dec/Jan 180/200 double calendar spread with AAPL trading at $189, we
have the better-looking risk/reward graph in Figure 6.6.

Now we have a more reasonable profit potential of about 30% if held
to about a week or so to expiration. But the risk/reward curves are still
drooping too much. We have a negative volatility skew here as well, but it
is smaller than the trade in Figure 6.5. In this trade, the call skew is −1.7
points (−2.6 points in Figure 6.5), and the put skew is only −0.7 points,
whereas it was −2.0 points for the trade in Figure 6.5.

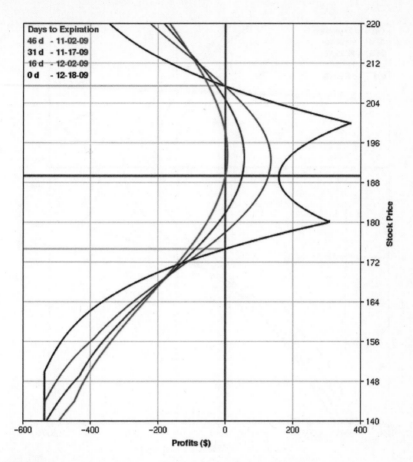

FIGURE 6.6 AAPL Dec/Jan 180/200 Double Calendar Spread
Source: Screenshots provided courtesy of Optionetics Platinum © 2010. All rights reserved, etc.

An excellent example of the trade setup we desire in a double calendar was the AAPL Nov/Jan $180/$200 call double calendar on October 14, 2009, shown in Figure 6.7.

Notice how the droop in the middle of the risk/reward curves has been eliminated. We have a broad break-even range of $173 to $210 and a potential gain of 35% if held to about a week before expiration.

Another good example is for Google on June 19, 2007, with GOOG trading at $514 and the Jul/Aug $490/$530 double call calendar at a debit of $940 and a break-even range from $478 to $550 (Figure 6.8). In this case, we have a positive volatility skew for both the calls (+0.9 points) and the puts

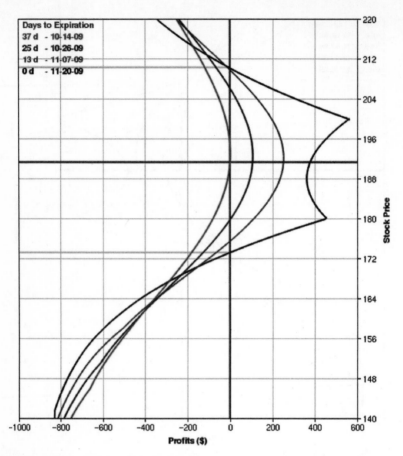

FIGURE 6.7   AAPL Nov/Jan 180/200 Double Calendar Spread
Source: Screenshots provided courtesy of Optionetics Platinum © 2010. All rights reserved, etc.

(+1.7 points). The positive IV skew has broadened the break-even range and increased the potential profitability.

DETERMINING THE OPTIMAL STRIKE PRICES

Positioning the strike prices of the double calendar spread involves trade-offs between the break-even range, the debit required to establish the position, and the estimated profitability. Once we have found a good candidate

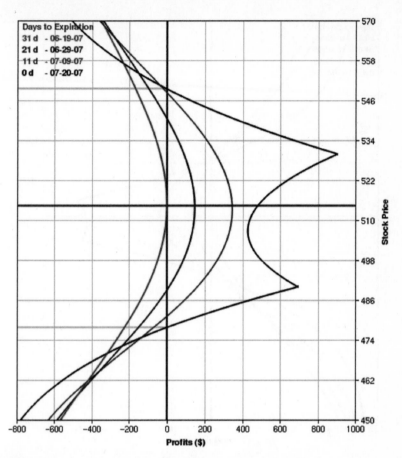

FIGURE 6.8 GOOG Jul/Aug 490/530 Double Calendar Spread
Source: Screenshots provided courtesy of Optionetics Platinum © 2010. All rights reserved, etc.

for the double calendar spread, we plot the risk/reward graph for varying strike prices, starting on either side of the stock or index price and moving farther OTM. Figures 6.9 through 6.12 show our search for the optimal strike prices for a double calendar spread on the Nasdaq 100 Index (NDX). As we broaden the strike prices, we decrease the debit and broaden our break-even range—both favorable trends—but our expected gain is decreasing. As we push the strike prices farther OTM, the risk/reward curves begin to droop in the middle and our profitability becomes negligible. Table 6.1 summarizes this search for the optimal strike prices for the NDX double calendar spread.

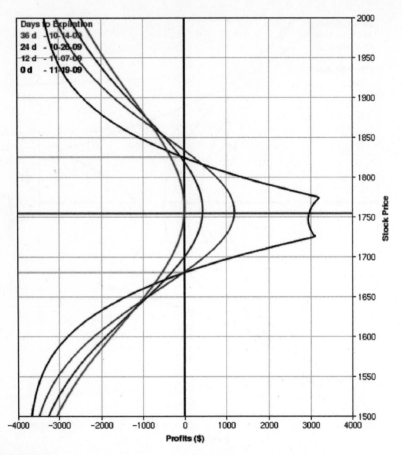

FIGURE 6.9 NDX Nov/Dec 1,725/1,775 Double Calendar Spread
Source: Screenshots provided courtesy of Optionetics Platinum © 2010. All rights reserved, etc.

The approach we use for finding a good candidate for the double calendar spread is very similar to what we had with the ATM calendar; the main difference is the search for the optimal strike prices. One other advantage of the double calendar spread is the broader break-even range that enables the position to handle the larger price moves of higher volatility stocks.

1. Sell about 25 to 30 days of time premium to maximize the time decay.

2. Check the current value of IV and its history over the past year. Be sure IV is in the lower 25% of its recent history. This is critical; if this condition isn't satisfied, stop here.

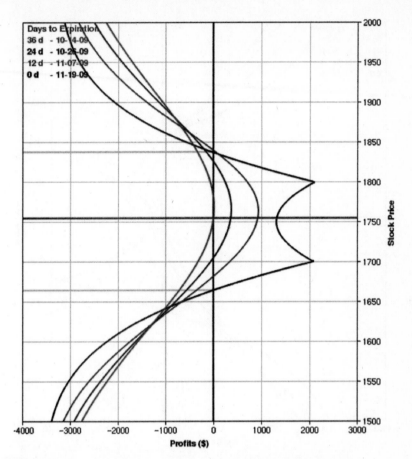

FIGURE 6.10 NDX Nov/Dec 1,700/1,800 Double Calendar Spread
Source: Screenshots provided courtesy of Optionetics Platinum © 2010. All rights reserved, etc.

3. Check the volatility skew:
   a. Don't trade a negative skew larger than one point.
   b. If the positive skew is greater than three to four points, investigate very carefully. The market is expecting something.
4. Calculate one standard deviation (σ) using the current ATM IV and the number of days to expiration for the front-month option being sold. Look at the price ranges (lowest to highest) over the past week and month. Avoid this stock if recent price moves have been larger than one σ.
5. Be sure no earnings announcements or other significant events are expected over the next 30 days.

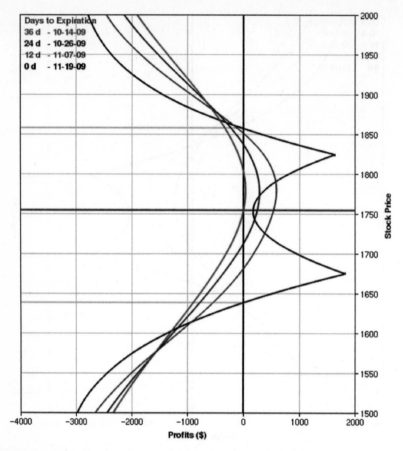

FIGURE 6.11   NDX Nov/Dec 1,675/1,825 Double Calendar Spread
Source: Screenshots provided courtesy of Optionetics Platinum © 2010. All rights reserved, etc.

6. Be sure you are selling at least $0.50 of time value in the front month; otherwise, trading commissions take too much of your profit.

7. Plot the risk/reward graph; experiment with different strike prices to find the optimum risk/reward graph. Ensure the break-even range will encompass any price movement you expect from this stock. Minimize or eliminate any droop in the risk/reward curve.

8. Estimate the likely return from the risk/reward graph if you close the trade one week before expiration. Be sure this is at least 30%. Disregard the maximum potential return at expiration; that return is unrealistic because we won't be taking the trade into expiration week.

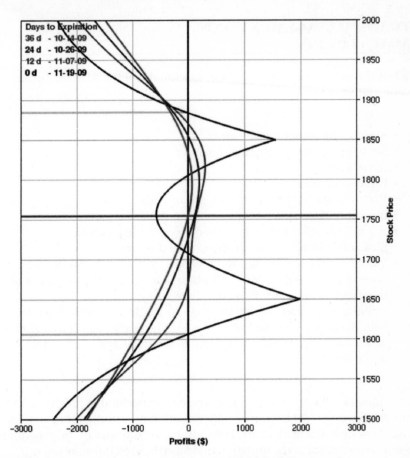

FIGURE 6.12 NDX Nov/Dec 1,650/1,850 Double Calendar Spread
Source: Screenshots provided courtesy of Optionetics Platinum © 2010. All rights reserved, etc.

TABLE 6.1 Trade-Offs with Strike Price Selection

Strike Prices	Break-evens	Debit	Estimated Return
1,725/1,775	$1,680–$1,825	$3,620	33%
1,700/1,800	$1,664–$1,837	$3,425	26%
1,675/1,825	$1,638–$1,858	$3,165	19%
1,650/1,850	$1,606–$1,884	$2,850	Negligible

TRADE MANAGEMENT AND ADJUSTMENTS

When the double calendar is initiated, write down the following points in your trading journal:

- Stock or index and the current price.
- Strike prices and expiration months.
- Initial debit.
- Break-even points.
- Volatility skews for the call and put spreads.
- Initial position delta.
- Implied volatility for each of the options in the position.
- Stop loss: use a 25% loss on the overall position.
- Volatility stop: if the implied volatility of the individual options decreases by more than two percentage points, close the trade. If a negative IV skew develops, close the trade.
- Adjustment trigger: divide the time to the front-month expiration in half; during the first half of the trade, trigger the adjustment at either strike price; during the second half of the trade, trigger the adjustment at the break-even prices.

Adjusting the double calendar involves considerable judgment. Once the trigger price has been tripped, evaluate the overall market trend and the stock or index price chart. Determine your estimate of the probability for a further move in the direction that has triggered the adjustment.

If your assessment is neutral to mildly bullish or bearish, then adjust by closing spreads on the offending side and opening new spreads slightly OTM. The new spreads should be call calendars if the stock or index is moving upward against your position or put calendars if it is moving downward. Determine the number to be rolled by modeling the trade with your options analysis software. Your objective is to cut the position delta in half.

If your assessment is strongly bullish or bearish, then close all of the spreads on the offending side and open new spreads above or below the current stock or index price. Position the new spreads based on your price prediction for the underlying stock or index.

If less than 10 days to expiration remain and the double calendar is between the front month and the next month, and the trigger for adjustment is tripped, simply close the trade. If the double calendar is over multiple months (e.g., a September/January spread), then make your adjustment as above, but roll out to the next month in the process.

As you begin to trade ATM calendars and double calendars, I recommend you trade them in a very simple way with no adjustments whatsoever. Follow the stop-loss and volatility stops, and treat the adjustment triggers as stops. This will close out trades more frequently, but will also greatly simplify the trade management process. As you gain experience, you can begin to adjust the positions as discussed if desired, but many experienced traders successfully trade these positions without adjustments.

MULTIPLE CALENDAR SPREAD POSITIONS

When you are adjusting your ATM and double calendar spread positions, multiple calendar spread positions will often result. When this happens, manage the resulting position by using the break-even prices as your adjustment triggers, reduce position delta with your adjustments, and keep position theta as large and positive as possible.

Another permutation of the double calendar strategy is to initiate the trade as a multiple calendar trade position. For example, one might build a position with an ATM call calendar spread, an OTM call calendar positioned near one standard deviation, and an OTM put calendar positioned near one standard deviation. As you manage and adjust this position, you may have calendar spreads positioned at several strike prices. In this situation, it is imperative that you manage the position by focusing on the overall position delta and theta values. With each adjustment, reduce delta back toward zero, but keep theta as large and positive as possible.

EXERCISES

1. Name the two principal risk factors for double calendar spreads.
2. What is the advantage of a double calendar over an ATM calendar?
3. When would you use an OTM call calendar instead of a double calendar?
4. I have chosen the strikes for my double calendar and the position delta is −$50. What does this tell you about my prediction for this stock?
5. I have a Jan/Apr $200 call calendar on AAPL. As we approach January expiration, AAPL is trading at $198. What are your choices?

6. If I am considering different strike prices for a double calendar on the Russell 2000 Index (RUT), what will change if I move the strikes closer together?

7. We established a Nov/Dec 110/130 double calendar on IBM with 30 days left in Nov, and IBM was trading at $120. IBM trades up to $130 over the next ten days. What should I do?

CHAPTER 7

Double Diagonal Spreads

The vertical spread was formed by buying and selling the options in the same expiration month. We can diagonalize that spread by buying and selling the two options in different months and at different strike prices. Similar to a double calendar spread, we may establish two diagonal spreads, one positioned above the current index or stock price, and one positioned below the current index or stock price. This is the *double diagonal* spread, a delta-neutral option trading strategy.

DIAGONAL SPREADS

All of the vertical spreads we studied earlier can be diagonalized, but, in practice, it is most common to diagonalize the bull call spread. In August 2009, IBM was trading at $120. Let's assume I had a long-term bullish outlook for IBM, so I bought the January 2010 $110 call for $13.75 and sold the September $120 call for $3.05, for a net investment of $10.70. I have effectively bought a call spread on IBM, stretched out over time. I would manage this trade by tracking the cost basis of the long call. The cost basis starts out at $10.70. As we approach September expiration, IBM is trading at $122, so we buy back the Sept call for $2.20 and sell the Oct $120 call for $4.60 for a net credit of $2.40. Now my cost basis in the Jan 2010 call is $8.30.

As we approach October expiration, IBM has traded up to $128 and the earnings announcement is imminent. We now have a choice. If I am bullish on IBM, I could buy back the Oct $120 call for $8.65 and sell the Nov $130 call for $3.25. That actually increases my cost basis to $13.70, but I have also expanded the spread to $20. Thus, I have increased my profit potential, assuming that IBM continues to trade strongly at or above $130. The conservative approach would be to roll out to November, but remain at the $120 strike price. So I buy back the Oct $120 call for $8.65 and sell the Nov $120 call for $9.60, reducing my cost basis in the Jan 2010 $120 call to $7.35. Note that we could have chosen to close the spread at this point, buying back the Oct $120 call for $8.65 and selling the Jan 2010 $110 call for $19.40, for a net profit of $2.45 (our cost basis was $8.30). Based on our original investment of $10.70, we achieved a 23% return.

But we chose to continue on with our trade. Now we are short the Nov $120 calls and long the Jan 2010 $110 calls and our cost basis is $7.35. IBM pulled back after the earnings announcement, but then traded up to $128 before the November expiration. We continued the trade by rolling out to December, buying the Nov $120 call for $8.28 and selling the Dec $120 call for $9.05. Our cost basis is now $6.58. Notice how our cost basis reduction is diminishing as IBM continues to trade above the strike price we have sold. When you are in a bull call diagonal spread and the underlying stock trades up strongly, the credit received for each month's roll will be smaller. Eventually, you are forced to close the trade for a profit (nothing wrong with that), or, if very bullish, you could roll out and up to the next strike price. This will increase the cost basis but it also increases the profit potential.

As we near December expiration in this example, IBM is trading at $129, and we could roll out to January for a credit of $0.45. This would reduce our cost basis to only $6.13, so we would most likely close the trade at this point rather than rolling to January. We would buy back the Dec $120 call for $8.85 and sell our Jan 2010 $110 call for $19.00, or a net credit of $10.15. Since our cost basis had decreased to $6.58, we have a gain of $3.57 or a 33% return on our original investment.

Note the power of this trade: IBM did trade up from $120 to $129, or 7.5%, but our diagonal spread gained 33% over about five months.

In summary, the diagonalized bull call spread is established and managed in the following way:

1. Establish the spread by buying an in-the-money (ITM) call in a future month and selling a call either at-the-money (ATM) or just out-of-the-money (OTM) in the front month.

2. As you approach expiration,

    a. If the stock price is below the strike price sold, allow the short position to expire worthless.

   b. If the stock price is near or above the strike price sold, roll out to the next month by buying back the short call and selling the same strike price call in the next month.

   c. If the stock price is above the strike price sold and you are strongly bullish on this stock, then roll out and up to the next strike price call. This increases the profit potential if the stock price continues upward, but it also increases your cost basis, making a pullback costly.

3. As your spread goes deeper ITM, the credit to roll out will diminish, and you will be forced to either close the spread for a profit or roll out and up to the next strike price to continue the trade.

4. If the stock pulls back, you could roll out and down to create a calendar spread, but analyze this carefully. If the stock price continues to fall, the position will continue to lose money. You may be better off to close the trade and move on.

Some traders use Long-Term Equity Anticipation Securities (LEAPS) options for their long-term stock investments. In those cases, one might occasionally sell OTM calls against the LEAPS options to reduce the cost basis over time. As we saw with the IBM example, if the stock price trades up strongly, you may be forced to close the position for a profit at some point as the credit to roll diminishes. If the trader is still bullish, he can simply buy a new position in the LEAPS at that point.

The diagonalized bull call spread is fundamentally a directional bullish strategy. But the diagonal spread can be used to build a delta-neutral trading strategy—the double diagonal spread.

DOUBLE DIAGONAL SPREADS

As mentioned earlier, we may diagonalize any vertical spread, but the diagonalized bull call spread is the most common variant of diagonal spreads. If we wish to create a delta-neutral strategy, we can place a diagonalized bear call spread above the current stock or index price and a diagonalized bull put spread below the current stock or index price. We would normally think of these as credit spreads, but the double diagonal is often a debit spread due to the high cost of the long options in the next month. However, this will also invoke a margin requirement from your broker, even though it is a debit spread. The margin requirement will vary from broker to broker, but commonly will be the value of the spread on each side; for example, two $10 diagonal spreads would have a margin requirement of $2,000.

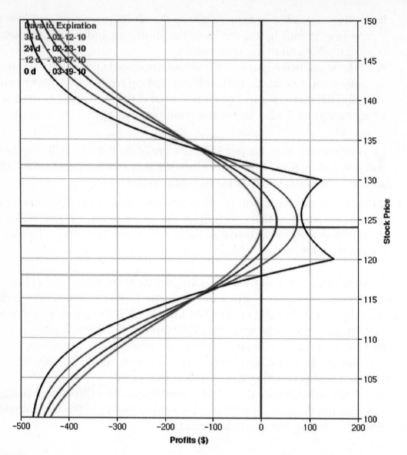

FIGURE 7.1   IBM Mar/Apr 115/120 125/130 Double Diagonal Spread
Source: Screenshots provided courtesy of Optionetics Platinum © 2010. All rights reserved, etc.

Figure 7.1 shows the risk/reward graph for a double diagonal on IBM on February 12, 2010, with IBM trading at $124. The general shape of the curve is virtually identical to the double calendar spread.

Establishing a double diagonal spread is also similar to the double calendar in the strike selection process. As we move the strikes OTM, the break-even range increases, but the risk/reward curves begin to droop in the middle and the potential profit decreases, as you can see in Figure 7.2.

The double diagonal is a delta-neutral trade and makes its money through its positive theta, or time decay, similar to the double calendar spread. The double diagonal is also a positive vega spread, but not nearly

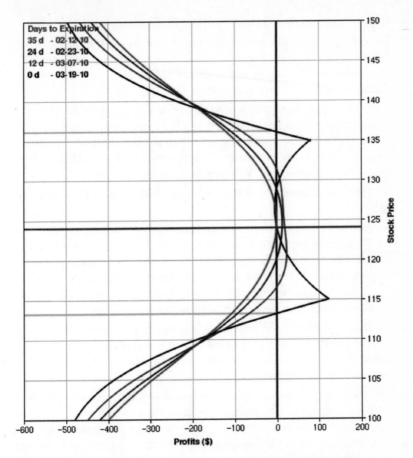

FIGURE 7.2 IBM Mar/Apr 110/115 135/140 Double Diagonal Spread
Source: Screenshots provided courtesy of Optionetics Platinum © 2010. All rights reserved, etc.

so large a positive vega as we have with the double calendar. So decreases in implied volatility (IV) are not as large a concern for the double diagonal.

Double diagonal spreads can be positioned on the broad market indexes as a monthly income generation trade. The general process for initiating and managing the trade is as follows:

1. Initiate the trade with about 30 to 40 days to expiration in the front-month options.
2. Sell the front-month call and put options at about one standard deviation OTM.

3. Buy the next strike OTM call and put in the next month.

4. Double diagonals are usually debit spreads due to the high cost of the future month options. But the double diagonal position will have a margin requirement, usually the width of the spread on each side of the trade, but this may vary with the broker.

5. Plot the risk/reward graph in your options analysis software and estimate the maximum gain if closed on the Friday before expiration week. Close half of the spreads whenever you achieve half of the maximum gain. Set your stop-loss at an overall position loss of 25% of the maximum loss computed by the options analysis software.

6. Trigger the adjustment if the index price touches either short strike price:

   a. Adjust by buying back the short option and selling the next option OTM, creating a calendar spread on that side of the position, or

   b. Adjust by selling the option at the strike price where we own the long option in the later month, and buy the option in the later month at the strike price we are short in the front month. This creates a double calendar spread on that side of the position.

7. On the Friday before expiration week, calculate the standard deviation (σ) for the front-month short options. If the short option is $\geq 2\sigma$ OTM, allow that option to expire worthless. If the short option is $< 2\sigma$ OTM, buy back those options.

8. After expiration, either close the remaining long options or create a new trade using one or more of those options. For example, one alternative may be to create an iron condor with the remaining long options (see Chapter 9). But if the index has moved very much in either direction, this may not be feasible.

MANAGING THE TRADE

The double diagonal spread can be used on the broad indexes as a very effective income generation trade. But one must carefully manage the risk to ensure long-term success with the double diagonal spread. And we will see that this is typical of all of the delta-neutral strategies.

The first key success factor is setting a maximum loss limit or target of 25%. Monitor the profit and loss of your position daily. Whenever the loss exceeds 25% of the risk capital, close the trade (you may approximate the capital at risk conservatively as the amount of one of the spreads plus the initial debit; e.g., two $10 spreads with a $560 debit would be $1,560 of capital at risk).

Double diagonals should be adjusted whenever the index price touches one of the short strike prices. Then the trader has a choice of two adjustments. One can create a calendar spread on the side being threatened by buying back the short option in the front month and selling the next strike higher or lower to create a calendar spread on that side of the trade. Alternatively, one can create a double calendar on the side being threatened by buying the same strike in the later month that we are short in the front month to create one calendar. The other calendar is then created by selling the option at the next strike up or down in the front month.

For example, assume the Russell 2000 Index (RUT) stands at $630 and we establish a Mar/Apr 590/600 put and 660/670 call double diagonal. If RUT trades up to $663, we can adjust in one of two ways:

1. Create a call calendar at $670 by buying back the short Mar $660 call and selling the Mar $670 call.
2. Create a double calendar at $660 and $670 by buying an Apr $660 call and selling a Mar $670 call.

Refer back to Chapter 6 on how to manage and adjust the calendar or double calendar spreads on this side of the position.

DOUBLE DIAGONALS VS. DOUBLE CALENDARS

Double diagonal spreads and double calendar spreads are both very effective delta-neutral income generation trades. Double calendar spreads are large positive vega positions; hence, decreasing IV is a significant risk for that position. By contrast, double diagonals have smaller positive vegas and are not nearly so sensitive to decreasing IV. Thus, in a low-volatility environment, one should favor the double calendar since increased IV will augment the profitability of the double calendar. In high-volatility environments where decreasing IV may be more of a risk, one should favor the double diagonal spread.

Double diagonals generally require more capital to be invested and this decreases the returns as compared to double calendars. Stated another way, double calendars have higher yields than double diagonals.

The double diagonal presents the trader with more alternatives for fine tuning and adjustment than the double calendar. However, that very flexibility carries additional complexity.

When comparing the double diagonal spread to the iron condor (Chapter 9), one disadvantage of the double diagonal is the margin requirement mandated by many options brokers. For a double diagonal with two $10 spreads, the margin requirement is commonly $2,000, whereas it would be $1,000 for the iron condor at most brokers. This effectively reduces the returns by half.

In my experience, double diagonals are less popular with income traders, who tend to favor iron condors, butterflies, and double calendars.

EXERCISES

Consult the options chains in Tables 7.1 and 7.2 for the following exercises.

1. Assume we just purchased five AAPL Jan 2011 $180 calls for $39.80. AAPL closed today at $193. We have 12 days left in December and

TABLE 7.1   AAPL December 2009 Options Chain

AAPL Dec 2009 Calls			AAPL Dec 2009 Puts		
Strike	Bid	Ask	Strike	Bid	Ask
170	23.55	23.70	170	0.25	0.28
175	18.75	18.90	175	0.46	0.48
180	14.20	14.35	180	0.87	0.92
185	10.05	10.15	185	1.71	1.75
190	6.55	6.65	190	3.15	3.20
195	3.90	3.95	195	5.50	5.60
200	2.17	2.18	200	8.75	8.85
210	0.56	0.57	210	17.05	17.25

TABLE 7.2   AAPL January 2010 Options Chain

AAPL Jan 2010 Calls			AAPL Jan 2010 Puts		
Strike	Bid	Ask	Strike	Bid	Ask
170	25.25	25.45	170	1.86	1.92
175	21.05	21.25	175	2.66	2.72
180	17.15	17.35	180	3.75	3.85
185	13.65	13.80	185	5.20	5.35
190	10.60	10.70	190	7.05	7.25
195	8.00	8.10	195	9.50	9.60
200	5.85	5.95	200	12.35	12.50
210	2.98	3.05	210	19.40	19.55

40 days in January. Consult the options tables and decide:

   a. Which option will you sell? Why did you choose that one?

   b. What is your cost basis in your LEAPS calls?

   c. Assume we decided to sell the Dec $190 call for $6.55. What is our cost basis in the Jan 2011 $180 calls?

   d. As we approach Dec expiration, AAPL is trading at $190.52. What should you do?

   e. As we approach Dec expiration, AAPL is trading at $188.21. What should you do?

   f. As we approach Dec expiration, AAPL is trading at $201.10. What should you do?

2. Assume we purchased three Jan 2011 $180 calls for $39.80. We sold three Dec $190 calls for $6.55, and they expired worthless. We then sold the Jan $190 calls for $4.25. As we near Jan expiration, AAPL is trading at $195. We roll our Jan $190 calls to Feb $190, for a net credit of $3.76. If our Feb calls expire worthless and the Jan 2011 $180 calls are sold at $35.83, what is our return?

3. As we approach Feb expiration, we are short the AAPL Feb $190 calls and long the AAPL 2011 $180 calls. AAPL has an earnings announcement tomorrow and you are bullish on AAPL. What should you do?

4. We wish to establish the Dec/Jan AAPL 170/180 put and 200/210 call double diagonal.

   a. What will it cost to establish ten contracts of this position?

   b. If AAPL trades above the upper break-even after ten days in the trade, what adjustment options are open to you?

   c. If AAPL closes at $195 at Dec expiration, and the Dec options expire worthless, describe two alternatives you have facing you. Which would you choose and why?

CHAPTER 8

Butterfly Spreads

A butterfly spread is created by selling two options and buying one option farther out-of-the-money (OTM) and one option farther in-the-money (ITM). The butterfly can be created with calls or puts. The two sold options are called the *body* of the butterfly, and the two long options are the *wings* of the butterfly. Butterfly spreads are quite versatile and may be used in speculative directional trading or for delta-neutral income generation trading.

AT-THE-MONEY AND OUT-OF-THE-MONEY BUTTERFLY SPREADS

If we establish a butterfly with calls, we have effectively put on two vertical spreads. The lower half of the butterfly is a bull call spread, while the upper half is a bear call spread; put another way, we have bought one call spread and sold another call spread where the calls sold in each spread are at the same strike price. Your online broker probably has a butterfly order screen where this entire position may be entered as a single order. Alternatively, you could enter two separate orders for the two vertical spreads that make up the butterfly spread.

We can create a butterfly spread with put options in the same way with one butterfly order or by selling the lower put spread (a bull put spread) and buying the upper put spread (the bear put spread). In this case, the puts sold in both spreads will be at the same strike price.

Figure 8.1 displays the risk/reward graph for a call butterfly spread on the Russell 2000 Index (RUT) on February 23, 2010, with RUT at $625. This example was constructed by buying three contracts of the March $690 calls and three contracts of the March $570 calls and selling six contracts of the $630 calls for a debit of $10,686.

The break-even range is quite broad, from $606 to $654. The maximum profit is found at the peak of the risk/reward curve at expiration, at $7,314 or 68%. But this is an unrealistic maximum profit since the index would have to settle precisely at $630 on expiration Friday for this to occur. A more likely maximum profit estimate is represented by the time decay line at eight days to expiration with a profit of about $2,000 to $3,000 over a range of the index price from approximately $615 to $640. Since we have positioned this butterfly roughly at-the-money (ATM), we refer to this as an *ATM butterfly spread*.

Figure 8.2 shows the same butterfly built with put options. The initial debit of $10,731 is very close to that for the call butterfly in Figure 8.1.

The break-even range of $606 to $654, maximum profit of $7,269, and the position Greeks are virtually the same for the two positions. The trader is normally indifferent to building the ATM butterfly spread from calls or puts; choose whichever yields the best price. If we increase the width of the butterfly wings by moving the long options farther out from the current index value, we will broaden the break-even range but also increase the initial debit and decrease the maximum profit.

The profitability of the ATM butterfly derives from the rapid time decay of the ATM options sold. ATM option time decay is most rapid during the last 30 days of the option's life, and that powers the profitability of the ATM butterfly. ATM butterflies are appropriate for stocks that are expected to trade within a relatively narrow channel over the next 30 days. Positioning the butterfly spread ATM on a broad market index like the Standard & Poor's 500 Index (SPX), the NASDAQ 100 Index (NDX), or RUT is a common way to use the butterfly as a delta-neutral income generation trade.

The butterfly spread may also be used as a speculative directional trade. Since call options increase in value as the underlying stock or index price rises and conversely for put options, one would place an OTM call butterfly above the current stock or index price to profit from a bullish prediction and an OTM put butterfly below the current stock or index price to profit from a bearish prediction.

OTM butterfly spreads can often be placed for relatively low investments, but they remain low-probability, high-risk trades. Some traders use OTM butterflies as their "what if I'm wrong" trades. For example, my prediction may be for Google to trade upward, and I position a bull call spread accordingly. But I might also enter an OTM put butterfly down below the current price of Google to help offset the loss of my call spread if Google

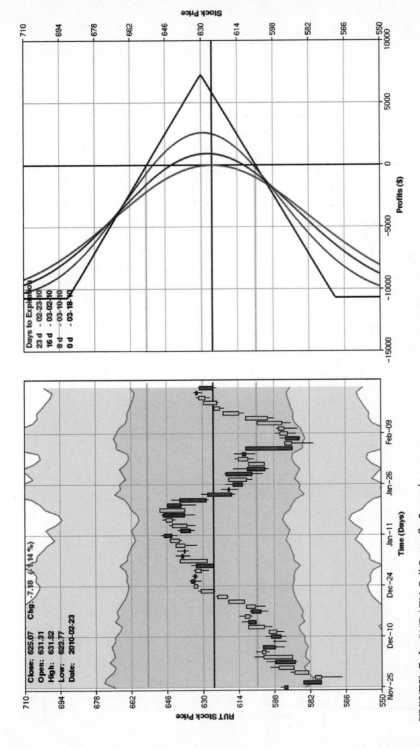

FIGURE 8.1 RUT ATM Call Butterfly Spread

Source: Screenshots provided courtesy of Optionetics Platinum © 2010. All rights reserved, etc.

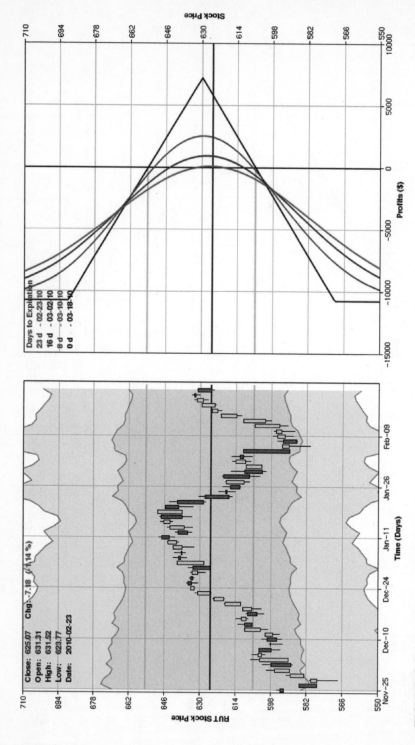

FIGURE 8.2 RUT ATM Put Butterfly Spread

Source: Screenshots provided courtesy of Optionetics Platinum © 2010. All rights reserved, etc.

falls rather than trading upward. The OTM butterfly serves as my inexpensive hedge for the call spread.

Butterfly spreads generally have small negative values of vega, so many traders use butterfly spreads as speculative trades around earnings announcements. The collapse of implied volatility after the announcement destroys a calendar spread, but it has a much smaller effect on the butterfly spread.

IRON BUTTERFLY SPREADS

We can use both calls and puts to create what is known as the *iron butterfly* by selling one call and one put at the same strike price ATM and buying one call OTM and one put OTM. In effect, we have sold a call spread just above the current stock or index price and sold a put spread just below the current stock or index price, where the short options in each spread are ATM at the same strike price.

If the wings of the iron butterfly are equidistant, the margin requirement will be based on the spread of the wing; for example, if our wings are $50 wide, the margin requirement will be $5,000 per contract. However, brokers have varying margin requirements; you should always confirm your broker's margin requirements before entering a trade.

The risk/reward graph for a RUT Mar 570/630/690 iron butterfly is displayed in Figure 8.3. The initial credit of $7,314 is the maximum profit; the maximum loss is $10,686, so the maximum return is 68%. The break-even range is quite broad, covering $606 to $654.

A comparison of the risks, rewards, potential returns, and break-evens of this iron butterfly to the call butterfly in Figure 8.1 and the put butterfly in Figure 8.2 shows that all three of these trades are virtually identical. This reinforces what we learned earlier: debit spreads and credit spreads positioned at the same strike prices will have virtually identical returns and risk/reward characteristics.

THE BROKEN-WING BUTTERFLY

If we unbalance the butterfly spread by making one of the wings wider than the other, we have created the *broken-wing* butterfly spread. Some refer to this as a *skip strike butterfly spread*. Recently, several books and advisory services have sprung up touting the broken-wing butterfly as the secret weapon of professional floor traders and market makers and therefore the "best options trading strategy." Of course, that is bunk. The broken-wing

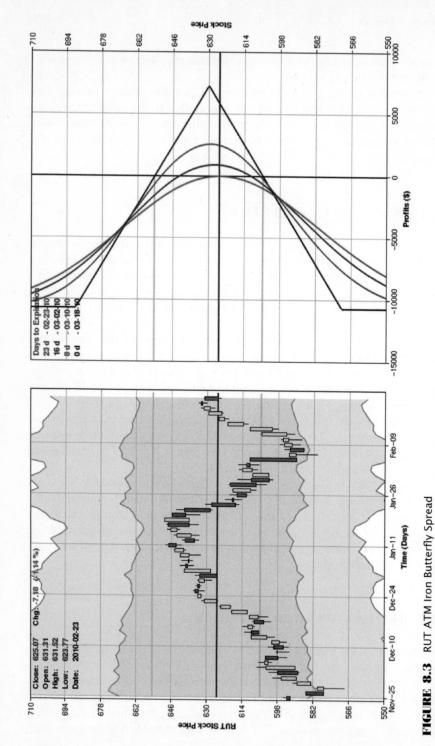

FIGURE 8.3 RUT ATM Iron Butterfly Spread

Source: Screenshots provided courtesy of Optionetics Platinum © 2010. All rights reserved, etc.

butterfly spread has advantages and disadvantages, like any other options strategy.

The risk/reward curve of the broken-wing butterfly spread has a bias to one side or the other. In many cases, my prediction for a stock or index price may be for it to trade in a narrow sideways range. But my analysis of the market may lead me to believe that if I am wrong, it will be to the downside. So my prediction is sideways with a lower probability of a price decline. This would be an example of a situation where a broken-wing butterfly might be the right trade.

In general, widen the wing on the side of the trade opposite the direction you think the underlying stock or index may trade. In the previous example, where I suspect the stock or index price may move down, I would skip one or two strikes on the upper half of the butterfly to bias the trade to the downside.

Figure 8.4 shows the risk/reward curve for an actual trade of a friend of mine on Google (GOOG) in August 2007. GOOG had appeared to have just bounced off support, and my friend established a ten-contract Sept $480/$500/$510 put butterfly for a net credit of $1,950. Broken-wing butterflies may be debit or credit spreads, depending on the particular situation.

The trader's prediction was for GOOG to trade sideways close to a price of $500. But by positioning the spread in this way, he would profit if GOOG in fact traded on up from the bounce off support. This trade would be profitable for any price of GOOG above $489 and would have its peak profit right at $500. By August 31, GOOG had traded up to $515 and my friend closed this trade for a $2,080 gain.

The obvious advantage of this trade is locking in a profit for any price of Google above $489. But we have paid for that advantage in two ways. First, our downside potential loss of $8,050 is greater than the downside or upside potential loss for a comparable ATM butterfly centered on $500. Second, this position has a margin requirement of $12,800 ($20,000 for ten $2,000 credit spreads less the $7,200 credit for the $480/$500 bull put spread; the position's net credit results from the $7,200 credit less the $5,250 debit from the $510/$500 bear put spread).

The broken-wing butterfly spread is an effective tool in the trader's toolbox when you encounter a situation such as the above example with Google, where we believe the stock or index will trade sideways, but we have a bias as to which direction the stock or index may trade if we are wrong.

MARGIN REQUIREMENTS

When the wings of the call or put butterfly spreads are equidistant from the body, there is no margin requirement for this trade. However, if the

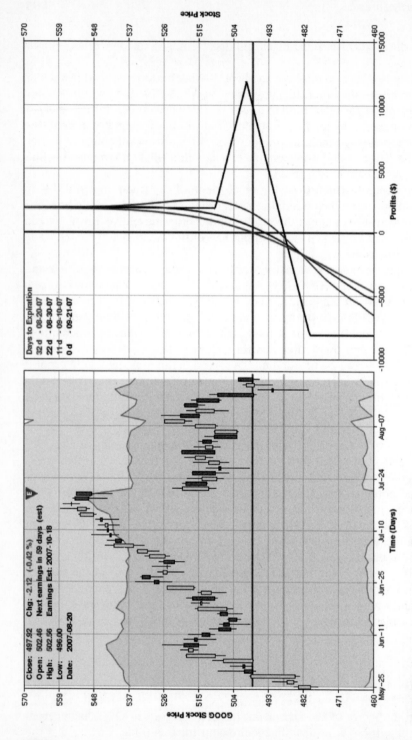

FIGURE 8.4 GOOG Broken-Wing Butterfly Spread

Source: Screenshots provided courtesy of Optionetics Platinum © 2010. All rights reserved, etc.

two sold options are pulled apart by even $5 or $10, the spread will incur a margin requirement for the credit spread side of the butterfly.

If we were to modify the butterfly in Figure 8.1 by shifting the upper call spread up to $640/$700, our wings are still the same width, but our sold calls are now at $630 and $640; this butterfly will now have a margin requirement of $6,000 per contract based on the $60 wings. This butterfly example was formed with three contracts, so the margin requirement would be $18,000. The initial debit would be $11,746, and the maximum profit would be about 53% (Figure 8.5).

Note that the risk/reward curve of this butterfly is more evenly positioned over the current value of RUT, but we have paid dearly for this adjustment with a higher debit, and we now have a margin requirement. Some would even call this a condor spread as soon as the sold strikes were separated. Actually, we have a continuum of trades between the extreme positions of the butterfly and the condor, and we will discuss that further with our focus on condor spreads in Chapter 9.

TRADE MANAGEMENT

The simplest way to manage the butterfly spread is to add extra options on the wings as the trade is established to make the position delta neutral. Then establish a hard stop-loss based on the overall loss of the position at any given time during the trade. I recommend a stop-loss of 20%. Close the trade for a profit either when the net gain is > 25% or on the Friday before expiration week. Many experienced traders manage their butterfly spreads in just this way, so simplicity should not be seen as inferior in any respect. To summarize this simple butterfly trade management approach:

1. Establish the spread around 30 days to expiration; fill one vertical spread at a time or use a butterfly order form.
2. Compare calls and puts to see which give you the best prices and returns.
3. Sell the ATM options and buy one option at one standard deviation (σ) OTM and one option at 1σ ITM (or, if using an iron butterfly, buy both options at 1σ OTM).
4. Be sure the wings are equidistant to establish a zero margin requirement; the iron butterfly always has a margin requirement.
5. Buy extra calls and/or puts on the wings to bring the position delta close to zero (i.e., delta neutral).
6. Close the trade when you are down 20%.

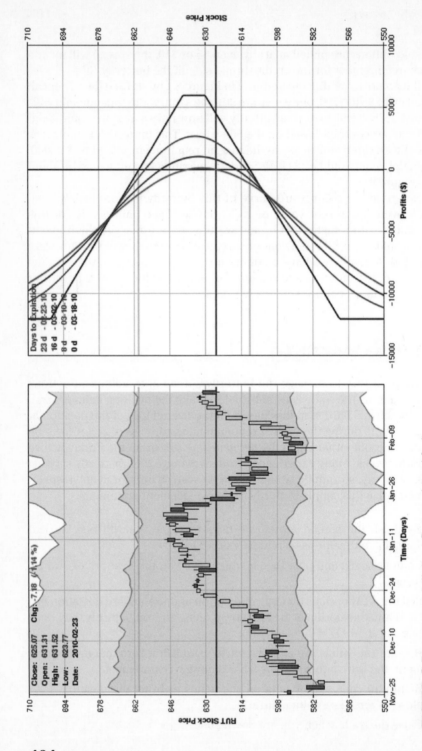

FIGURE 8.5 RUT ATM Call Butterfly Spread (Modified)

Source: Screenshots provided courtesy of Optionetics Platinum © 2010. All rights reserved, etc.

104

7. Close half of the contracts in the trade and take your profit if you are up ≥ 25%.

8. Close the trade on the Friday before expiration week.

One may add adjustment criteria to increase the possibility of larger returns, but at the cost of larger possible losses (no free lunch). If the stock or index price reaches either break-even price, then we need to adjust the position with the goal of reducing delta closer to zero by closing spreads on the threatened side of the position; for example, if the index has moved down and reached the lower break-even price, we would close the appropriate number of call debit spreads (or put credit spreads in the case of a put butterfly) to reduce delta at least by half. If more than 15 days remain to expiration, one could establish an equal number of new call debit spreads with the short call at or near the current value of the index. This more advanced butterfly trade management approach is summarized below:

1. Establish the spread around 30 days to expiration; fill one vertical spread at a time or use a butterfly order form.

2. Compare calls and puts to see which give you the best prices and returns.

3. Sell the ATM options and buy one option at one standard deviation (σ) OTM and one option at 1σ ITM (or, if using an iron butterfly, buy both options at 1σ OTM).

4. Be sure the wings are equidistant to establish a zero margin requirement; the iron butterfly always has a margin requirement.

5. Buy extra calls and/or puts to make the trade delta neutral.

6. Close the trade when you are down 25%.

7. If the stock or index price hits either break-even, and less than fifteen days are left until expiration, close the trade. Otherwise, adjust the trade: Cut position delta in half by rolling the appropriate number of spreads up or down. For example, if the index has moved up to the upper break-even of my call butterfly, I buy back one of the ATM calls and sell one of the OTM calls. Then I sell one call near the current index price and buy one call farther OTM.

8. Close the trade on the Friday before expiration week.

The experienced trader will immediately see other equally viable adjustment techniques. For example, one might simply buy back one of the short calls and sell a call at the current value of the index. Or you could close some of the spreads on the threatened side without making any other trades; this will reduce the potential losses on that side while allowing time decay to continue to work in your favor.

An example of an ATM butterfly spread from one of my personal accounts is illustrated in Figure 8.6. This position was established on January 12, 2010, with ten contracts of the RUT.

RUT calls were positioned at the strikes of 610/640/670, for a debit of $8,500. The break-even prices of $619 and $662 represented my trigger prices for adjustment. The RUT fluctuated up and then down over the next ten days, but tripped the lower break-even price on January 22, 2010 (Figure 8.7). The trade is on the borderline of moving into a loss at this point, so either closing the trade or initiating an adjustment is in order.

Figure 8.8 shows the trade after we have sold five contracts of the 610/640 calls. Notice how we have dramatically lowered the maximum loss if the index continues to trade downward, but we retain an opportunity for a profit if the index levels out or pulls back.

About a week later, the index bounced back upward, and I took that opportunity to close the trade for an 18% gain ($1,480) in 16 days (Figure 8.9). The advantage of the adjustment was limiting our downside risk while we patiently waited for the index to either trade sideways or rebound back upward. Without the adjustment, I would have closed the trade for a $650 loss when the RUT broke through the lower break-even price.

This trade also illustrates another critical success factor of trading: don't look back and second guess yourself. In this example, I closed the trade on January 27, 2010, for a $1,480 gain, but one week later, I could have closed that butterfly spread for a $2,785 gain. Develop your trading system and follow your rules. It is important to post-audit your trades to learn and improve. The danger is that you use "looking in the rearview mirror" as an excuse to continually modify your trading rules from month to month. This erodes your trading discipline and consistency, and may cause you to not follow your rules at some point in the future and result in a large loss.

CLOSING BUTTERFLY SPREADS

Closing butterfly spreads can be a little confusing, especially if you have made adjustments to the trade and no longer have a simple butterfly. As you either approach a time stop, like the Friday before expiration week, or have hit a stop-loss trigger, it is important to analyze the position for the various closing possibilities. For example, if the index has traded up strongly and broken the upper break-even of your call butterfly spread and you have decided to close the position, you could close the entire butterfly

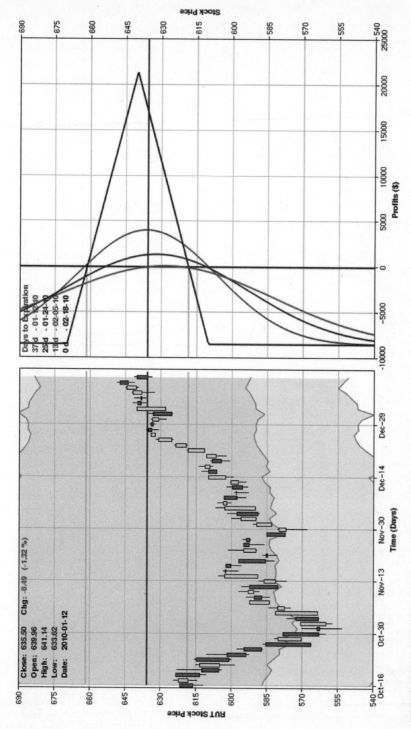

FIGURE 8.6 RUT ATM Call Butterfly Spread (1/12/10)

Source: Screenshots provided courtesy of Optionetics Platinum © 2010. All rights reserved, etc.

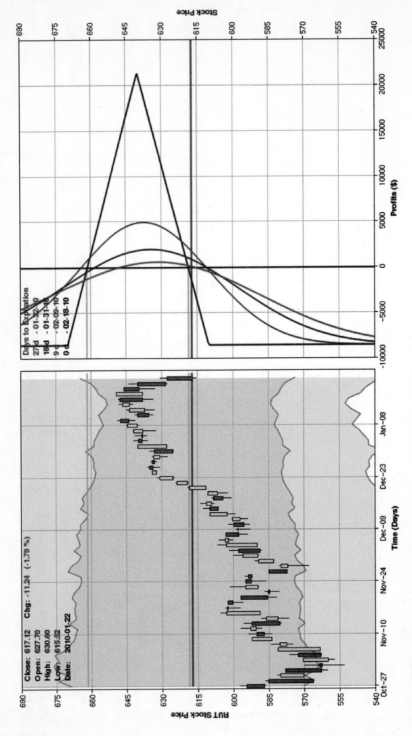

FIGURE 8.7 RUT ATM Call Butterfly Spread (1/22/10) before Adjustment

Source: Screenshots provided courtesy of Optionetics Platinum © 2010. All rights reserved, etc.

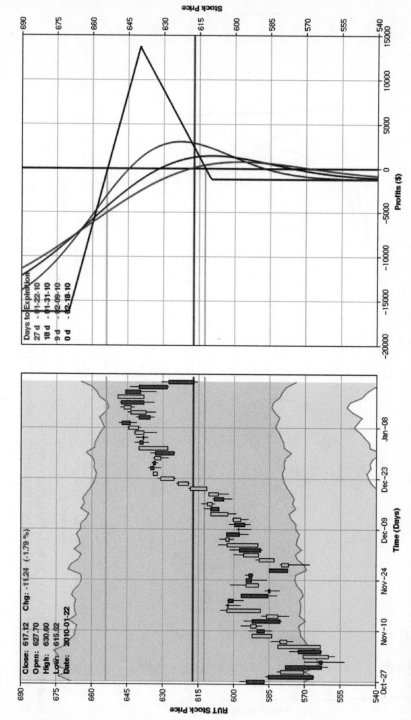

FIGURE 8.8 RUT ATM Call Butterfly Spread (1/22/10) after adjustment

Source: Screenshots provided courtesy of Optionetics Platinum © 2010. All rights reserved, etc.

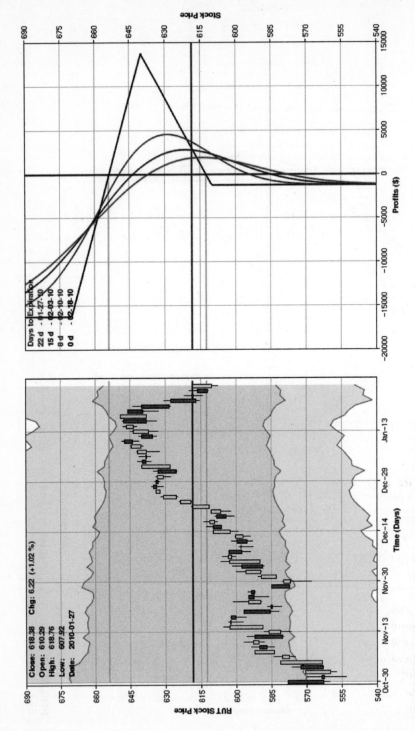

FIGURE 8.9 RUT ATM Call Butterfly Spread (1/27/10)

Source: Screenshots provided courtesy of Optionetics Platinum © 2010. All rights reserved, etc.

with a butterfly order, just entering all of the trades in reverse (the "buy to opens" become "sell to closes," etc.). Another alternative is to close only the portion of the butterfly that is in trouble, that is, the bear call spread. So you could enter an order to buy back the bear call spread half of the butterfly spread and allow the bull call spread portion to expire ITM.

When closing either side of a butterfly spread, remember that one-half of the butterfly is a debit spread without a margin requirement, but the other side is a credit spread that would have a margin requirement if it were standing alone. If I close the debit spread side of my butterfly spread, I may be surprised to see that a margin requirement has been imposed on the account, possibly limiting the capital available for other trades and adjustments.

In summary, always break down your butterfly spread position into the vertical spread components. This will allow you to better envision the trades required to close the position. When adjustments have not been made to the position, using the broker's butterfly spread order form to close the entire position may be the simplest and best alternative.

BUTTERFLY SPREADS AS ADJUSTMENTS

Butterfly spreads are very versatile trades. They can be placed OTM as directional trades with great profit potential if the trader's prediction is correct and they may be used as delta-neutral nondirectional trades. Many traders also use OTM butterfly spreads as their "what if I am wrong" position to lessen their losses if a trade turns against them. They make relatively inexpensive hedges.

When you are trading a directional vertical spread, and the stock moves against you, consider the possibility of converting the vertical spread into a butterfly to salvage a gain or at least minimize the loss. For example, if I buy a $450/$460 call spread on GOOG when it is trading at $480, I may consider this to be a reasonably conservative trade. But what if GOOG pulls back to $465? If my prediction is that GOOG will stabilize and trade back up, I may choose to hold my call spread. But if $460 is a solid support level and I believe GOOG is likely to trade sideways at or just above $460, then converting my vertical spread into a butterfly may be an excellent adjustment for this position. I could sell the $460/$470 call spread for a credit; now I have a $450/$460/$470 butterfly spread that will have a reasonably broad range of profitability.

However, there are always trade-offs. By converting my vertical spread into a butterfly spread, I have increased the capital at risk in this position. Thus, my judgment of GOOG's likely price action is critical. I may be well advised to simply close the vertical spread for a loss and move on to another trade.

In the next chapter we will discuss condor spreads and many condor traders use OTM butterfly spreads for protection in the event the underlying stock or index moves against their position.

EXERCISES

1. On January 28, 2009, GOOG closed at $349. A trader is considering the following spreads:

   a. Jan 2010 400/450/500 call butterfly
   b. Mar 330/350/370 call butterfly
   c. Mar 300/320/340 put butterfly

   What would you infer was the trader's expectation for GOOG if he were to establish each of these trades?

2. Based on the Jan 2010 options chain in Table 8.1, compute the initial credit or debit and the margin requirement for each of the following RUT spreads with RUT at $598:

   a. Jan 570/600/630 call butterfly
   b. Jan 570/600/630 iron butterfly
   c. Jan 570/600/630 put butterfly
   d. Jan 550/600/620 call butterfly

TABLE 8.1   RUT January 2010 Options Chain

Jan 2010 Calls			Jan 2010 Puts	
Bid	Ask	Strike Price	Bid	Ask
54.70	55.60	550	8.30	8.70
46.50	47.30	560	10.20	10.50
39.10	39.70	570	12.70	13.10
32.10	32.60	580	15.60	16.00
25.70	26.20	590	19.10	19.50
20.00	20.40	600	23.40	23.90
15.10	15.50	610	28.40	29.00
11.00	11.30	620	34.30	34.90
7.70	8.10	630	41.00	41.70

3. What is the Jan 550/600/620 call butterfly called? What would be your price prediction if you established this spread?

CHAPTER 9

Condor Spreads

A condor spread is used when the trader expects the stock or index to trade within a sideways or slowly trending channel over the life of the trade. The condor's profitability is driven by time decay's effect on the two spreads as time passes and the stock or index price remains within the channel formed by the two vertical spreads. A condor spread can be created with call or put options, or both in the case of the iron condor spread.

THE BASIC CONDOR SPREAD

The trader establishes a condor spread when he opens two vertical spreads and positions one down below the current stock or index price and one up above the current stock or index price. In Figure 9.1, the price chart for Apple Computer (AAPL) is displayed as of November 12, 2009. I drew the horizontal support and resistance lines at $186 and $208.

AAPL traded sideways in a range of approximately $182 to $188 in late September before decisively breaking through on October 6. But notice how AAPL traded down to $186 on October 19 before breaking out to form a new high at about $208 on October 23 and 24. Then AAPL traded back down and touched support at $186 three days in succession in late October and early November. If you were looking at this price chart you might very logically predict that AAPL will trade within the channel formed by $186 and $208 over the next month.

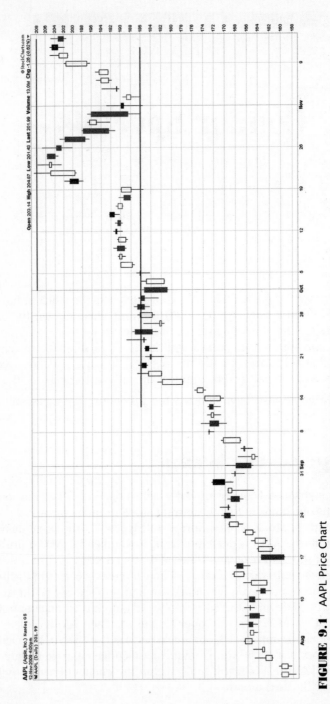

FIGURE 9.1 AAPL Price Chart

Source: Screenshot provided courtesy of StockCharts.com © 2010. All rights reserved.

114

Based on this prediction, we could sell the December $210/$220 call spread by buying the Dec $220 call for $1.94 and selling the Dec $210 call for $4.30, for a net credit of $2.36 or $236/contract. This defines the upper limits of the channel defined by the resistance level at $208. We could reasonably expect AAPL to trade up as high as $208 before meeting resistance and bouncing back lower.

We could define the lower limits of the channel by establishing the Dec $175/$185 call spread by buying the Dec $175 call for $28.30 and selling the Dec $185 call for $19.35, for a net debit of $8.95 or $895/contract. After observing the strong support level at $186, we are using this spread to predict that AAPL will trade down as low as $186 before bouncing off support and trading higher.

These two vertical spreads comprise a condor spread. This spread is named after the North American Condor, a large bird with wingspans that can approach ten feet. The condor spread on AAPL above covers a price range of $25 from $185 to $210; as long as AAPL trades within this channel before the December option expiration, this position will be profitable. This wide range of price chart covered by the condor is the basis for this seemingly unusual name for an options spread.

This AAPL call condor would have cost $659 to establish (the $895 debit for the lower spread less the $236 credit for the upper spread). If AAPL closed at a price within this channel defined by these two spreads, the total profit would be $341 or 52% ($105 maximum profit for the $175/$185 call spread and $236 maximum profit for the $210/$220 call spread). We could also have constructed a condor at these same strike prices for AAPL using put options; in that case, we would have a credit spread below the stock price and a debit spread above the stock price.

Table 9.1 illustrates the basic equivalence of the condor spreads created with calls or puts. Condors constructed with either all calls or all puts will have essentially identical levels of maximum profit and maximum loss.

Figure 9.2 displays the risk/reward graph for the AAPL Dec 175/185 210/220 call condor we developed as an example.

Notice the wide break-even range for this trade. This chart illustrates an important aspect of the trader's mind-set when establishing this trade. We approached this example with AAPL by concentrating on the price chart and levels of support and resistance. One could augment that approach with other technical indicators, but this approach selects the strike prices for the spreads based on a prediction of the likely trading range derived from a price chart analysis.

An alternative approach is one that simply considers AAPL's price movement as a random walk. The shaded areas on the price chart of Figure 9.2 are the areas encompassed by plus and minus one and two standard deviations. Some traders will use a probability calculation to position

TABLE 9.1 AAPL Condor Spreads

Expiration Month	Strike Price	Option Type	Credit or (Debit)	Maximum Profit (%)
December	175	Calls	($28.30)	
December	185	Calls	$19.35	
December	210	Calls	$4.30	
December	220	Calls	($1.94)	
		AAPL December Call Condor:		$341 (52%)
December	175	Puts	($1.17)	
December	185	Puts	$2.32	
December	210	Puts	$12.20	
December	220	Puts	($19.90)	
		AAPL December Put Condor:		$345 (53%)

the condor spread. In this example, the trader who was using a probability calculation might have positioned the call spreads one strike higher at $220/$230. Then the condor spreads would be roughly encompassing the area of price movement of plus or minus one standard deviation, yielding a probability of success for this trade of about 84% (refer back to Chapter 2). This would have resulted in a condor spread with an even wider break-even range, but it would also have reduced the maximum profit potential.

The risk/reward graph for this $175/$185 and $220/$230 condor is illustrated in Figure 9.3. The break-even range has expanded by 25%, but the debit for the trade has increased to $789, and the maximum potential return has been reduced to 27%. Compare Figures 9.2 and 9.3. Notice the better balance of the risk/reward curve in Figure 9.3 around the price of AAPL, but also note that the break-even prices in Figure 9.2 encompass the recent price movement of AAPL very well.

There is not a right or wrong about these two approaches to the condor spread. In general, it is probably more common for the technical price analysis approach to be used on individual stock condors, while traders who apply condor spreads to the broad market indexes tend to use a probabilistic approach.

THE OPPORTUNISTIC MODEL

The condor spread illustrated with Apple Computer in the previous section is an excellent example of what I will refer to as the *Opportunistic Model* for condor trading strategies. When the trader analyzes the price chart of

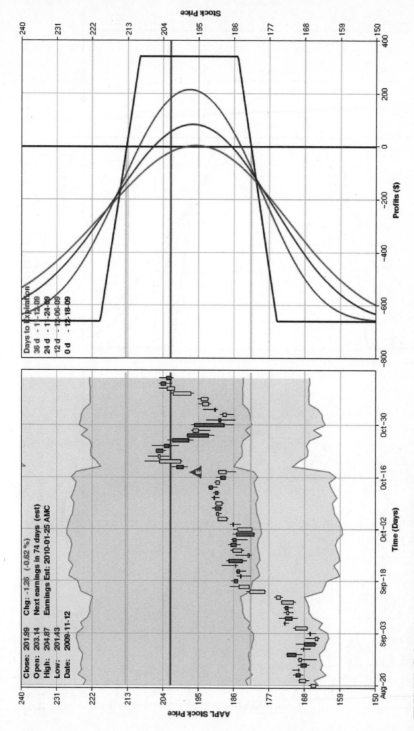

FIGURE 9.2 AAPL 175/185 210/220 Condor Spread

Source: Screenshots provided courtesy of Optionetics Platinum © 2010. All rights reserved, etc.

117

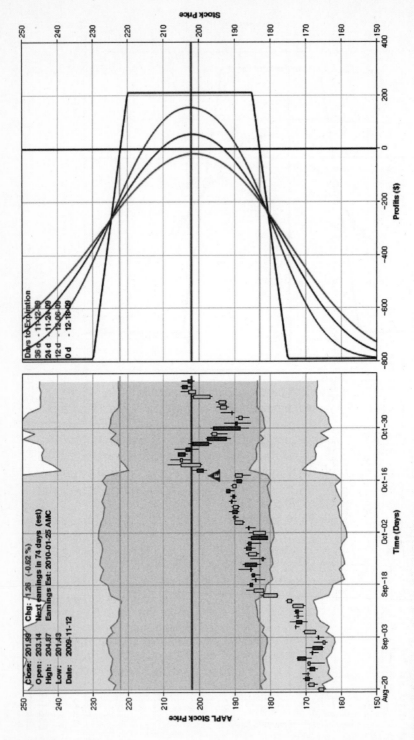

FIGURE 9.3 AAPL 175/185 220/230 Condor Spread

Source: Screenshots provided courtesy of Optionetics Platinum © 2010. All rights reserved, etc.

a stock and observes a tight trading range over the past few weeks or perhaps even months, it may be an excellent candidate for a condor spread. Relatively simple technical analysis using levels of support and resistance may be employed, as well as more sophisticated technical indicators. Many stock-scanning tools can be found on brokerage web sites and are also contained in stock and options analysis software. These tools may be configured to scan for stocks whose recent price behavior appears to be trading within a price range or channel. The process for establishing condor spreads within the Opportunistic Model is as follows:

1. Look for stocks you expect to trade within a channel for the next 30 days.

2. Calculate one standard deviation (σ) for the underlying stock with the current at-the-money (ATM) implied volatility (IV) and the number of days to expiration. Look at the stock's price chart; has it moved more than one σ in the past several weeks?

3. Look at historic levels of IV and compare with the current IV. Is the market expecting large price swings?

4. Look for levels of support and resistance on the price chart; place the short strikes of your spreads above resistance and below support.

5. Close the trade when the position loss exceeds 20%.

6. Close the trade when the current gain is $\geq$ 50% of the maximum potential profit.

7. Close the trade on the Friday before expiration week.

More sophisticated trade management and adjustment techniques for the condor spread will be covered in detail in later sections of this chapter.

THE INSURANCE MODEL

Many traders use the condor spread on broad market indexes with what I refer to as the *Insurance Model*. This is the probabilistic approach to the condor strategy. In this model, one positions his condor spreads each expiration month based on probability calculations; for example, one approach might be to always place the short strikes of the spreads just outside one standard deviation out-of-the-money (OTM). Consider the analogy to the auto insurance business:

- *Frequency.* The auto insurance agent will sell policies every month; he won't stop offering policies when a winter storm is approaching.

Similarly the condor trader will establish his condor positions every month based on consistent criteria of risk and return. This trader is not attempting to predict which months will be good months for trading the condor strategy.

- *Premiums.* The premiums for auto insurance are based on statistical measures of risk for the driver. Thus, a teenage boy will pay more for his insurance policy than a 40-year-old family man. The condor trader will receive credits consistent with the risk he is comfortable assuming for the trade; placing the spreads closer to the current value of the index will return larger credits and potentially larger gains, but also incurs a higher risk for the trade.

- *Reserves.* The insurance company will set aside a portion of the premiums collected as a reserve to pay out on policies based on the statistical expectations of risk for the policyholders; those reserves will be sufficient to pay claims but will be only a fraction of the total premiums received. A system of adjustment techniques and stop losses will serve the condor trader in a similar way by controlling losses to be a small percentage of gains and thus keep the condor strategy profitable over time.

The process for establishing condor spreads within the Insurance Model follows:

1. Choose one of the broad market indexes, for example, Standard & Poor's 500 Index (SPX), Russell 2000 Index (RUT), Nasdaq 100 Index (NDX), etc.

2. Develop and consistently apply a probabilistic model to select strike prices; for example, calculate $\pm 1\sigma$ and position the short strikes of the call and put spreads at or just beyond 1σ.

3. Consistently use a similar time to expiration; for example, always initiate the position at 45 to 50 days to expiration.

4. Settle on an adjustment methodology, including trigger criteria. Adjustment techniques will be discussed in detail later in this chapter.

5. On the Friday before expiration week, close any spread that is $< 2\sigma$ OTM. Allow spreads that are $> 2\sigma$ OTM to expire worthless.

Trading condor spreads within the Insurance Model is an excellent method of generating a steady income from your account. We will discuss the trade-offs inherent in many of the preceding choices later in this chapter (e.g., initiating the condor at 30 days vs. 50 days to expiration).

IRON CONDOR SPREADS

The iron condor spread is a simple variation on the traditional condor spread; if we sell a call spread above the stock or index price for a credit and also sell a put spread below the stock or index price for a credit, we have created an iron condor spread. When we discussed vertical spreads in Chapter 4, we noted that the debit spread and the credit spread at the same strike prices will have virtually identical levels of risk and reward; so there is no inherent advantage to either spread.

This is also true when we compare and contrast condor and iron condor spreads. On March 11, 2010, with the RUT at $672, IV = 20.1%, and 35 days to April expiration, I established two condor spreads positioned at ± 1σ. One was created with call options at $620/$630 and $710/$720 for a net debit of $723. The other was an iron condor created with a credit put spread at $620/$630 and a credit call spread at $710/$720. Figure 9.4 displays the risk/reward graph for the debit call condor, and Figure 9.5 displays the risk/reward graph for the iron condor at the same strike prices.

The risk/reward graphs are absolutely identical. Both trades have break-even prices of $627 to $713; the iron condor has a maximum profit of $272 for a 37% return; the debit call condor has a maximum profit of $277 for a 38% return. But the iron condor does have one significant advantage.

When I establish a debit spread, my maximum profit can be achieved when both options are ITM at expiration; then my broker will exercise both options, leaving the amount of the spread in my account. Consider this example: I bought a bull call spread on IBM at $120/$130 for $850 and IBM closes on expiration Friday at $135. My short $130 calls will be exercised against me, requiring me to sell 100 shares of IBM at $130. My broker will exercise my $120 calls on my behalf, buying 100 shares of IBM at $120 and turning around and selling those shares at $130 to satisfy the exercise of my short $130 calls. That leaves the spread between $120 and $130, or $1,000, in my account (less commissions). After subtracting the debit required to establish the spread of $850, I have my net profit of $150. So a debit condor will always incur the commissions for four legs to establish the trade, and four more commissions to close the trade, although in some instances, the credit spread half of my debit condor may be allowed to expire worthless.

And that brings us to the advantage of the iron condor. As we approach expiration week, the index price may be two or more standard deviations from either, or perhaps both short options. If that is the case, we can safely allow those options to expire worthless and save those trading

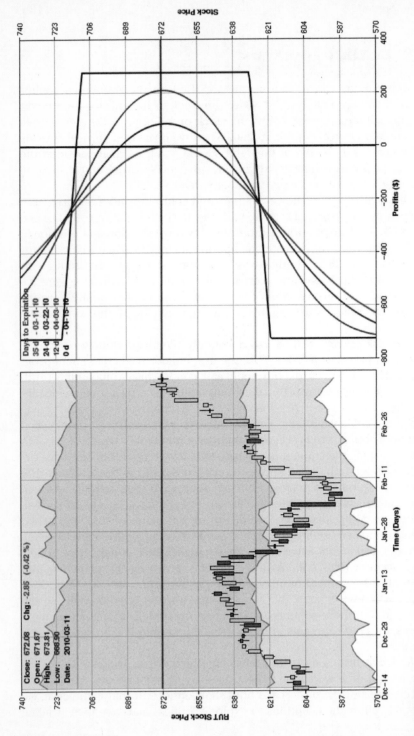

FIGURE 9.4 RUT 620/630 710/720 Call Condor Spread
Source: Screenshots provided courtesy of Optionetics Platinum © 2010. All rights reserved, etc.

122

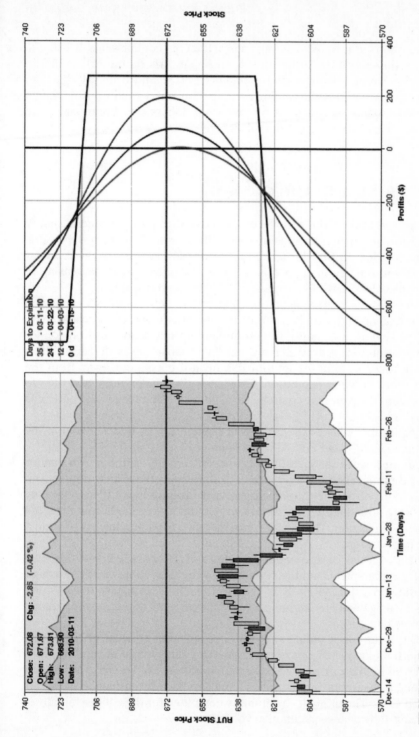

FIGURE 9.5 RUT 620/630 710/720 Iron Condor Spread

Source: Screenshots provided courtesy of Optionetics Platinum © 2010. All rights reserved, etc.

123

commissions. But we actually save more than the commissions. It will typically require $0.20 to $0.30 to close those spreads on the Friday before expiration week even when the spread is far OTM. So we are saving $20 to $30 per contract plus the trading commissions every time we can allow a spread to expire worthless. A few hundred dollars saved here and there adds up. That is the iron condor advantage.

VEGA RISK AND THE CONDOR

Condor and iron condor spreads are negative vega positions; increasing IV decreases the value of the position while decreasing IV increases the value of the position. In Chapter 6, we discussed the vega risk of the calendar spread, but the risk is the opposite for the calendar spread: increasing IV helps the calendar while decreasing IV hurts its profitability.

We showed in great detail in Chapter 4 the effects of IV changes on the vertical spread. Condors simply consist of two vertical spreads, so increased IV does not change the profitability of our condor or iron condor at expiration, but it does make it harder to close the trade early. When IV increases, it shifts the interim risk/reward curves out away from the risk/reward curve at expiration. Thus, at a given index price and time to expiration, the gain that could be realized by closing the spread early has been diminished.

Figure 9.6 displays the risk/reward graph for an iron condor on the RUT at $580/$590 and $700/$710 on January 19, 2010 with RUT at $649.

About a week later, RUT had dropped to $618, and this iron condor stood right at break-even (Figure 9.7). But notice the effect of increased IV in Figure 9.8, where the same position is displayed with IV increased by 25%. Note how the interim risk/reward curves have pulled away from the curve at expiration. The position has dropped from break-even to almost $900 underwater.

The vega risk of the condor presents itself commonly in just this way: the index plummets, and the condor is losing value simply on the basis of the price drop, but normally IV rises as the market drops, so our position is also losing value due to increased IV. This results in our position taking a double hit.

But if the index pulls back or trades sideways to close at expiration within the channel of our condor, then we achieve the maximum profit displayed by the risk/reward curve at expiration. So the vega risk is very real and measurable, but it applies to us only if we are forced to close our spread early. The ultimate profitability computed for the condor initially is unchanged by changes in implied volatility.

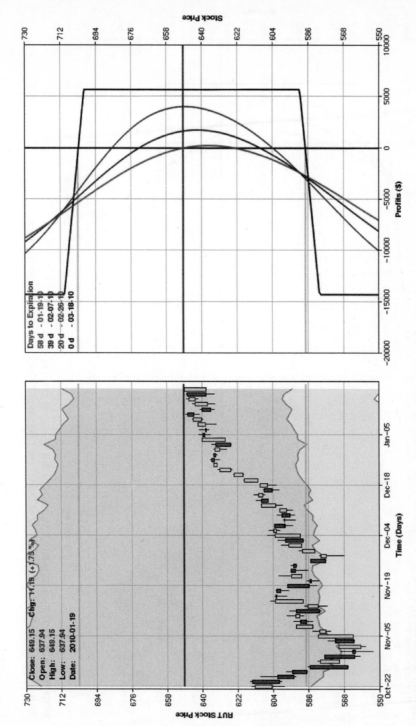

FIGURE 9.6 RUT 580/590 700/710 Iron Condor Spread (1/19/10)
Source: Screenshots provided courtesy of Optionetics Platinum © 2010. All rights reserved, etc.

125

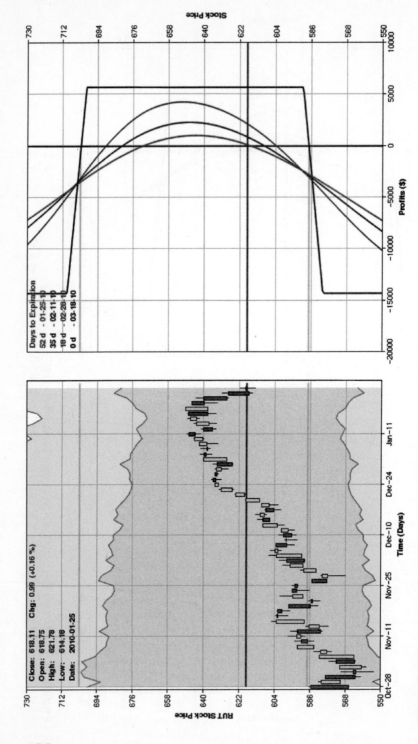

FIGURE 9.7 RUT 580/590 700/710 Call Condor Spread (1/25/10)

Source: Screenshots provided courtesy of Optionetics Platinum © 2010. All rights reserved, etc.

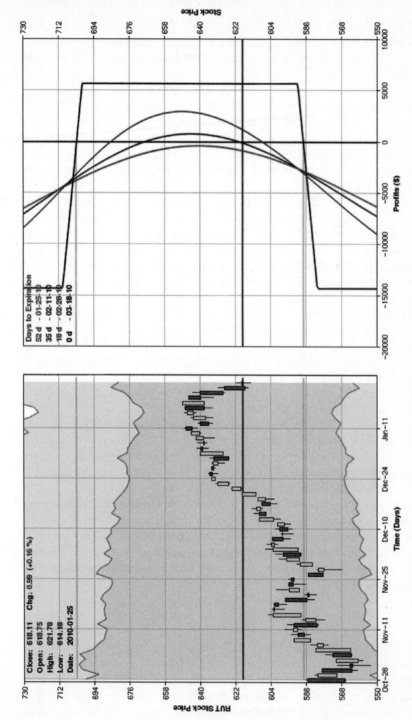

FIGURE 9.8 RUT 580/590 700/710 Call Condor Spread (1/25/10) with Increased IV

Source: Screenshots provided courtesy of Optionetics Platinum © 2010. All rights reserved, etc.

A related question is this: Should we favor establishing our condor when IV is high so we can receive larger credits and improve our returns? The short answer is no.

A trader commonly establishes the iron condor in one of three ways. He may calculate one standard deviation and place the spreads with reference to that price, or he may consistently sell the option with a particular delta value; for example, he looks through the calls and the puts for the strike prices where delta ≈ 10. And other traders choose the spread farthest OTM where they can still receive a minimum credit, for example, $0.85.

Increased IV is effectively self-correcting for the iron condor trader. When IV is high, the prices of the individual options are higher and the credits received will be larger. If I position my spreads based on a minimum credit, I will observe that my spreads will be farther OTM when IV is higher. But that doesn't mean the position is safer because increased IV tells us the market is expecting wider swings in price in the near future.

If I position my spreads with a standard deviation calculation, then the increased IV is taken into account by that calculation and results in a larger standard deviation, and the spreads are positioned farther OTM. Again, the increased IV was accommodated automatically by the increased standard deviation calculation.

If we think of delta as an estimate of the probability of the option's expiring in-the-money (ITM), then it makes sense that higher IV would correspond with higher deltas for the individual options. As IV increases, the probability of any particular option's expiring ITM has also increased. Hence, the trader who positions his iron condor spreads based on the delta of the short option has already incorporated increased IV into the positioning of his spreads.

Therefore, the condor trader is indifferent to the levels of IV when establishing his position. However, if IV is increasing as the index threatens one side of the trader's condor, the profit and loss position will be damaged by both the price move of the index and the negative vega of the condor. But the ultimate profitability of the condor at expiration is unchanged by the increased IV.

THE SHORT-TERM IRON CONDOR

The two principal parameters open to selection when establishing the iron condor position are time to expiration and the distance of the spreads OTM. One common configuration is the short-term iron condor, also known as the *low-probability iron condor*. The general procedure for establishing this position is:

1. Use options with 25 to 30 days to expiration and position the short strikes at $\sigma < 1.0$ (or $\Delta \sim 18$ to 25).

2. Enter the orders one spread at a time, starting at the midpoint of the bid/ask spread and working down from there. Be patient. Look at the market trend over the past hour; you might lead the market with your order; that is, if the market were trending downward, I might enter my put spread credit limit order $0.10 above the midpoint and let the market come to me.

3. Conservative approach: enter both spreads within a few minutes or use a condor order.

4. Aggressive approach: enter the call spread on strong bullish days and the put spread on weak bearish days. The risk of this approach is that the market may continue to trend in that direction and you do not have the opposite position to help compensate for the losses as the market moves against you. I have used this approach in the past but was burned too often, so I now follow the conservative approach of placing both the call and put positions within a few minutes of each other.

5. Enter your contingency stop-loss order for closing the put spreads in the case of a sudden market crash (this will be discussed further below).

6. Write down your trade plan: adjustment points; adjustment technique; stop-loss (contingency order); profit exits; time stop (these topics will be discussed further below).

7. Monitor the trade and adjust as necessary; close the trade according to your plan.

The probability of success for the short-term iron condor will be on the order of 60% to 65%, but this lower probability comes with a higher average rate of return. Rates of return will vary widely, but realized average returns for the short-term iron condor should range from 20% to 35%. Another advantage of the short-term iron condor is its short trade duration. Commonly, one may close the short-term iron condor in 10 to 15 days, and less time exposed to the market equals less risk.

THE LONG-TERM IRON CONDOR

The long-term iron condor is also known as the *high-probability iron condor* because it is usually established with a probability of success in the range of 85% to 90%. The general procedure for establishing this position is:

1. Use options with 45 to 50 days to expiration and position the short strikes at $\sigma > 1.0$ (or $\Delta \sim 7$–10).
2. Enter the orders one spread at a time, starting at the midpoint of the bid/ask spread and working down from there. Be patient. Look at the market trend over the past hour; you might lead the market with your order; that is, if the market were trending downward, I might enter my put spread credit limit order at or just below the ask price and let the market come to me.
3. Conservative approach: enter both spreads within a few minutes or use your broker's condor order screen.
4. Aggressive approach: enter the call spread on strong bullish days and the put spread on weak bearish days. The risk of this approach is that the market may continue to trend in that direction, and you do not have the opposite position to help compensate for the losses as the market moves against you. I have used this approach in the past, but was burned too often, so I now follow the conservative approach of placing both the call and put positions within a few minutes of each other.
5. Enter your contingency stop-loss order for closing the put spreads in the case of a sudden market crash (this will be discussed further below).
6. On the Friday before expiration week, compute σ for the index using the current IV and 6 days to expiration. Close either spread if it is $< 2\sigma$ OTM. If either spread is $> 2\sigma$ OTM, monitor those spreads closely over the next week; if they remain $> 2\sigma$ OTM, then allow them to expire worthless.
7. Write down your trade plan: adjustment points; adjustment technique; stop loss (contingency order); profit exits; time stop (these topics will be discussed further below).
8. Monitor the trade and adjust as necessary; close the trade according to your plan.

The higher probability of success for the long-term iron condor is naturally accompanied by a lower average rate of return, usually about 10% to 15%. The longer trade duration is a disadvantage in that the market has more time to move against your positions; however, your spreads are farther OTM and should be safer. Since the credits collected initially are smaller for the long-term iron condor, one will have to take the long-term iron condor nearly to expiration to collect the majority of the potential profit.

CAPITAL MANAGEMENT

One can trade the short-term iron condor every expiration month, making capital management much simpler. Determine the number of contracts to be traded by taking 85% of the capital in the account and dividing by $1,000. Then round down to the next integer. For example, if the account balance is $43,500, 85% is $36,975. After dividing by $1,000 and rounding down, we will trade 36 contracts in this account each month. The remaining capital is reserved for possible adjustments.

Capital management for the long-term iron condor is slightly more complicated. In any given month, we will have two condors in play, one for the current expiration month and one for the next expiration month. Determine the number of contracts to be traded in each expiration month by taking 40% of the capital in the account and dividing by $1,000. Then round down to the next integer. This will give you the number of contracts to be played in each expiration month. The remaining capital is reserved for adjustments.

The only way this is a reasonable capital allocation is if robust risk management is applied to this trading system. The maximum possible loss of the iron condor must be constrained via our risk management system to a reasonable number; that is, the maximum loss must be contained to be no more than the initial credit for the position. We will discuss this further in the next section.

RISK MANAGEMENT

Risk management for the iron condor strategy consists of a written plan with three essential components:

- Stop-loss orders placed as automated contingent orders with the broker.
- A specified adjustment technique and the value of the index that will trigger that adjustment.
- Criteria for closing the position after the adjustment has run its course.

The stop-loss order should be placed immediately after establishing the condor position. For the long-term condor, the stop-loss trigger is the value of the index where the delta of the short put option is estimated to be approximately 35. Determine this value by opening the option chain and looking at which put option currently has a delta of approximately 35. Take the difference between that strike price and the current value of the index and add that to the short put option strike price of the condor put spread. This is the trigger value for the stop-loss order.

For example, we have established the $1,080/$1,090 put and $1,220/$1,230 call iron condor on SPX while it was trading at $1,150. We look at the SPX option chain and see that the $1,125 put option has a delta = 33. We would place the stop loss trigger at $1,115 (the $1,125 put is $25 below the current value of SPX, so we add $25 to the short put strike of $1,090 to get $1,115).

We will discuss several possible adjustment techniques in the next section. For now, note that whatever adjustment technique will be used should be written in the trading plan at the initiation of the trade; don't try to decide what adjustment technique you will use in the heat of the battle.

The final component of the risk management plan is knowing when to throw in the towel and close the trade for a loss. This will be discussed further, but the bottom line is this rule: when the delta of the short option of either spread exceeds 30, close the position.

ADJUSTMENT TECHNIQUES

The probabilities of success are on your side when trading the condor or iron condor spread. Probabilities of success for the long-term condor will be of the order of 85% to 90%. However, it is worth noting that the probability calculation we have discussed is the probability of the index price's closing at expiration within the channel formed by the two spreads. If we were to calculate the probability of the index price's touching either short strike price before expiration and then pulling back into the channel, we would observe much lower probabilities of success. Stated another way, the probability of the index price's closing within one of our condor spreads at expiration is pretty small, but the probability of the index price's touching one of the spreads and then pulling back into the channel is much higher.

What this means in practice is that the index will move far enough in either direction to cause our position to go into the red far more often than we might have expected based on the probabilities of success calculated based on the closing price at expiration. Therefore, we need to be able to adjust our position to limit the damage when these extreme price moves occur. Several possible adjustment techniques are possible, each with its own advantages and disadvantages. These adjustment techniques are essential to the condor trader's long-term success.

The 200% Rule

The simplest adjustment technique is the 200% rule. As the trader monitors the iron condor position daily, he checks the debit to close each of the credit spreads. Whenever the debit to close the spread is greater than twice the original credit received when the spread was opened, the trader closes all of the spreads on that side of the condor. This is the simplest adjustment technique for the iron condor, and it is also the most conservative. Usually, the iron condor is established with similar credits on each side of the position. If we close one side for twice what we received, we should be roughly at break-even; we are underwater by approximately the amount of the credit received on one side, and presumably will profit by approximately the same amount on the other side of the condor. So this adjustment technique should result in break-even results or small losses in the worst-case scenario.

Closing Spreads

Another simple adjustment technique is to close a portion of the spreads as the index price approaches that position. The conservative trader should close 30% to 40% of the contracts when the delta of the short options in the spread exceeds 16. More aggressive traders could wait until delta hits 18 to 20. If the index price continues to move against the position and the delta of the short option is > 30, all of the remaining spreads on that side should be closed. The principal advantage of the closing spreads adjustment is that it reduces the maximum loss early.

The Buyback

When the index price moves against our position enough to shift the delta of the short options in our spread to 16 or more, we should buy back some of the short options to unbalance those spreads. If the index price continues in that direction, our position now has more long options that are gaining in value, thus partially compensating for the mounting losses from the remaining spreads. Buying back one short option for every ten spreads is the optimal adjustment, but you could increase that ratio to as many as 3 for every 20 contracts. We will discuss fine-tuning this adjustment in the next section of this chapter. If the index pulls back, the trader can then sell the appropriate number of options to reestablish the spreads.

The Long Hedge

The adjustment technique that I personally use most often for the iron condor is the long hedge. The adjustment is triggered by the short option's delta, just as in the closing spreads and buyback adjustments. When the short option delta exceeds 16, buy the option at the short strike price in the next expiration month. For example, if my position has RUT March $690/$700 call spreads and the delta of the $690 calls has hit 17, I would buy one or more of the April $690 calls. The scaling is similar to the buyback adjustment with the optimal long hedge adjustment being about one long hedge option for every ten contracts in the condor. A variation on the long hedge adjustment is to buy an ATM option in the expiration month of the condor's options. These options are more expensive, but fewer are required to hedge the position, because the ATM hedge option has a larger delta and thus effects a stronger adjustment to the position. The optimum adjustment with an ATM hedge option is about one long hedge option for every 20 contracts in the condor position.

ADJUSTMENT PROS AND CONS

Each of these adjustments reduces delta back closer to delta-neutral, but also reduces the positive theta for the position. The buyback and long hedge adjustments require additional capital to be invested into the position; this is adding risk to the position. The biggest advantages of the buyback and long hedge adjustments are their effects of flattening the risk/reward curve; that is, as the index price continues to move against the position, a flattened risk/reward curve translates to a smaller increase in the position losses with further index price moves. This is the result of the hedge options gaining in value as the index continues to move against the position and the spreads lose value.

The 200% rule is the simplest iron condor adjustment technique, and it is the most conservative adjustment. It would be difficult to incur a sizable loss using the 200% rule. In months where the index moves against one side of the iron condor and that side is closed at twice the original credit, a loss approximately equal to the credit has been generated. But the credit on the other side of the iron condor should be close to that loss in magnitude, resulting in a break-even or minimal loss.

The closing spreads adjustment reduces delta effectively and does not damage the positive theta too badly. It also reduces the maximum loss on the side of the iron condor that is under stress.

The principal advantage of the long hedge and the buyback adjustments as compared to the other adjustment techniques is allowing us to buy time for the index to pull back or trade sideways and consolidate; this may allow a trade to be salvaged for a gain when it would have been closed under one of the other adjustments. The buyback adjustment reduces delta, but it tends to damage the positive position theta more than the other adjustments. The short options that were closed in the buyback contributed a large portion of the position's positive theta, and this results in the theta damage. The risk/reward curves are flattened by the buyback adjustment, reducing further losses if the index price continues to move against the position. If the index pulls back, the trader can then sell options to reestablish the spreads on that side.

The long hedge adjustment does the best job of flattening the risk/reward curves. The practical effect of those flattened curves is to minimize position losses while we wait for a possible pull back. If the index does not pull back, we will close the trade anyway, but have held our losses to a minimum. If the index does pull back, we can sell the long hedge option(s) and still be in the trade for a potential gain that month. Thus, we will be able to salvage a gain in situations where the trade would have been closed with simpler adjustments. The disadvantage of the long hedge and buyback adjustments is the additional capital required by these adjustments. We are effectively putting more capital at risk in either case.

The long hedge and buyback adjustments will both be very effective in reducing the position delta back closer to zero, or delta-neutral. Both adjustments damage the position's positive theta value, but the long hedge reduces it less since the long options in the next month have smaller negative theta values.

As one begins to trade the iron condor, I recommend the 200% rule as the simplest and most conservative adjustment technique. More experienced traders should use the long hedge adjustment.

ADJUSTMENT CASE STUDIES

In this section we will compare and contrast the adjustment techniques for the iron condor strategy during some very difficult months for this strategy over the past couple of years. The first trade is an iron condor spread on the RUT, starting on February 5, 2010, with March options with 41 days to expiration and the RUT trading at $593. This was one of the worst months for iron condor traders in recent history. The winner was not the one who gained the most in this case; it was the one who lost the least. I used the Optionetics Platinum software for the backtesting; all spread prices were

TABLE 9.2 Iron Condor Adjustments I

Date	Adjustment	New Delta	% Change	New Theta	% Change	Net Result
2/16/10	200% rule	N/A		N/A		−$700
2/12/10	Closing spreads	−$54	−44%	+$78	−26%	−$2,080
2/12/10	Buyback	−$62	−35%	+$76	−28%	−2,750
2/12/10	Long hedge	−$45	−53%	+$77	−27%	−$2,220

computed from the midpoints of the bid/ask spreads. End-of-day data was used for option prices and the Greeks of the position.

The Mar RUT $510/$520 put and $650/$660 call iron condor was established on February 5, 2010, with 20 contracts for a credit of $2,800. On February 12, 2010, the delta of the $650 call was 17, tripping our adjustment trigger at delta > 16 for the closing spreads, buyback, and long hedge adjustments. The 200% rule triggered on February 16, 2010, with a debit to close the calls for $1.75.

The RUT index continued to trade upward, until the delta of the $650 calls closed at 38 on March 1, 2010. Then all of the call spreads and hedge options, if any, were closed. The put spreads were greater than two standard deviations OTM, so they were allowed to expire worthless. On February 12, 2010, the position stood at a net loss of $640, position delta = −$96, and position theta = +$105. The results after the adjustments are summarized in Table 9.2. The net results for the position after each of the adjustments and after closing on March 1 are also summarized in Table 9.2.

In this example, the 200% rule was the best adjustment in terms of limiting risk—it held the trade to a small loss of $700. Of the other three adjustments, the closing spreads adjustment fared slightly better than the long hedge, but one has to remember the trade-offs between these adjustments. During some months, the index will move against your position and trigger the adjustment, but then it may pull back. When it pulls back, the long hedge options can be sold and the full position is still in play; you have salvaged the trade. Also note that the long hedge adjustment was the most powerful in its reduction of the position's delta risk, whereas theta damage was approximately the same for the closing spreads, buyback, and long hedge adjustments.

Backtesting is a valuable exercise, but the results can be deceiving; we should be careful not to draw our conclusions from one specific backtest result. Often, the programs use end-of-day data that may skew the results from how you would have actually traded the position during market hours. To ensure fairness and objectivity, I chose two more "bad" months for the iron condor; the first simulates opening 20 contracts of the August

TABLE 9.3 Iron Condor Adjustments II

Date	Adjustment	New Delta	% Change	New Theta	% Change	Net Result
7/15/09	200% rule	N/A		N/A		−$560
7/15/09	Closing spreads	−$71	−39%	+$64	−26%	−$3,400
7/15/09	Buyback	−$72	−38%	+$53	−39%	−$3,270
7/15/09	Long hedge	−$56	−52%	+$57	−34%	−$2,750

RUT $390/$400 put and $550/$560 call iron condor on July 8, 2009 for a credit of $5,200 with RUT trading at $480. By the close of trading on July 15, the RUT had moved up sufficiently for the delta of the $550 call to be 22, past our adjustment trigger of 16. The 200% rule was also triggered with a debit to close the calls of $1.75. At the close on July 15, the position delta = −$116 and position theta = +$87. We applied all of our adjustments on July 15 and then closed the call spread trades on July 23 when the RUT had a huge $17 increase and the delta of the short $550 calls went to 47. The puts were assumed to have expired worthless. The results are summarized in Table 9.3.

The 200% rule again minimized the loss for this trade best of all of the adjustment alternatives. Similar to the first hypothetical trade, the long hedge adjustment had the strongest reduction in delta risk; since the 200% rule closes all of the spreads on the side under stress, it does not have a delta reduction (or you could say it is a 100% reduction in price risk). In the previous example, theta damage from the adjustments was approximately equal. In this example, theta damage by the buyback and long hedge adjustments was significantly worse than the closing spreads adjustment. But the long hedge adjustment minimized its loss significantly better than the closing spreads and buyback adjustments. In this example, the index moved so far and so fast that the long hedge options gained significantly.

The next "bad" month goes back to the crash of 2008. We will simulate establishing the RUT Oct $660/$670 put and $810/$820 call iron condor for a $5,200 credit with 20 contracts on September 2, 2008; the RUT was trading at $739. On September 15, the 200% rule was tripped and the 660/670 put spreads were closed for $3.10; the calls were allowed to expire worthless and the trade resulted in a loss of $1,000. The other adjustments were triggered earlier on September 4 when the delta of the $670 put was 23, position delta = +$36, and position theta = +$92. The results of the adjustments are summarized in Table 9.4.

In this example, the buyback and long hedge adjustments performed the best and salvaged gains for this period of time. However, the long hedge outperformed the buyback, in part because it damaged the positive theta

TABLE 9.4   Iron Condor Adjustments III

Date	Adjustment	New Delta	% Change	New Theta	% Change	Net Result
9/15/08	200% rule	N/A		N/A		−$1,000
9/4/08	Closing spreads	+$9	−75%	+$75	−18%	−$1,301
9/4/08	Buyback	−$10	−128%	+$39	−58%	+$580
9/4/08	Long hedge	−$20	−156%	+$48	−48%	+$920

of the position less than the buyback adjustment. One could also conclude that the long hedge adjustment enables the trader to be more aggressive and allow the index to run farther before giving up on the trade; the long options in the next month help hold the losses to a minimum while waiting for the pull back.

These examples, coupled with my experience trading the iron condor, underscore three principal recommendations with respect to iron condor adjustment techniques:

- The 200% rule is the simplest and most conservative adjustment and should be used by beginning condor traders and more conservative traders.
- The long hedge is the most effective advanced adjustment in that it allows us to salvage more trades for a gain.
- No one of these adjustment techniques will always be the best adjustment in every market circumstance.

One scenario wasn't covered in the preceding backtesting. In many cases, the index will move against our position sufficiently to trigger our adjustment but then pull back into the center of the channel formed by our condor. The long hedge adjustment will shine in those situations. We will sell our long hedge options for a small loss (the cost of the insurance) and play out the position for a net gain close to the maximum potential gain of the position.

MANAGING THE IRON CONDOR WITH THE GREEKS

The Greeks are very important parameters for the options trader. As we are monitoring a trade in progress, the Greeks allow us to see where our principal risk lies as we move forward.

In general, our risk from any options trade comes from three areas:

- A change in the price of the underlying stock or index
- A change in the implied volatility of the underlying stock or index
- The passage of time

Our trade position delta gives us a quantitative measure of the effect of a change in the price of the underlying stock or index. If my iron condor on SPX has a position delta of +$50, that tells me that a $5 move upward for the S&P 500 tomorrow will increase my position's value by $250; conversely, a $5 move downward will decrease my position's value by $250. Remember that a negative value of position delta reverses this relationship—a downward move in price would increase the position value and an upward price move would decrease the position value.

The vega value for our position communicates the risk associated with changes in implied volatility. Iron condor positions are always large negative vega positions, so rising IV will decrease the iron condor position's value. However, as was discussed above, this does not play a significant role in our management of the iron condor position.

Iron condors are positive theta positions. Assuming the index price and IV remain constant, our position will gain in value from the passage of time. The profitability engine of the iron condor position is the time decay measured by the position's positive theta value and it will increase as we near expiration. Thus, our objective is to adjust our condor position to minimize any losses due to stock or index price movement while we allow time decay to work for us to generate a profit.

As you monitor your iron condor position on a daily basis, track the ratio of position theta to position delta (ignore the signs of the numbers). The larger the theta/delta ratio is, the healthier our position is. As the underlying price moves against your position, the theta/delta ratio will decrease and may even decrease to less than one (i.e., delta is larger than theta). This is a signal that an adjustment may be required, or if an adjustment has already been applied to the position, this diminished theta/delta ratio indicates the adjustment is losing its effectiveness and the trade may soon have to be closed.

Monitor delta and theta as you adjust the iron condor position. Your objective in the adjustment is to reduce delta (a good target is to reduce delta by half) while keeping theta positive and as large as possible. You will find that a strong adjustment that takes delta back to zero will destroy most or all of the positive theta of the position. So the objective is to reduce your price risk as much as possible (as measured by delta) without destroying your potential profitability (as measured by theta). Whenever theta nears zero or goes negative, close the position.

ADVANCED ADJUSTMENT TECHNIQUES

After you have several months to a year of iron condor trading experience, you may consider rolling spreads as an additional adjustment technique. Rolling spreads adds to the capital at risk in the position, so it must be handled carefully and knowledgeably.

After our adjustment trigger point has been reached and we have placed the adjustment, we monitor our position Greeks and also the delta of the short option on the side of the condor that is under pressure. If our position theta becomes smaller than our position delta, this is a warning sign. When the short option delta exceeds 30, it is time to close the spreads on this side of the condor. If you are using the long hedge adjustment, leave the long hedge in place if you are planning to roll the spreads up or down to a new position. If rolling spreads will not be used, then close the spreads on the side under pressure and sell the long option(s). As long as the other spreads remain $> 2\sigma$ OTM, allow those spreads to expire worthless.

If 20 or more days remain to expiration, you may consider rolling up or down to open new spreads to continue the trade. Position the new spreads about 1σ OTM. Aggressive traders will increase the number of contracts used in the new spreads to compensate for some or all of the losses in closing the old spread position. But remember that this adjustment is increasing the amount of capital at risk in the trade. Use this technique with caution. I no longer use this scaling-up technique in my personal accounts.

The conservative trader will leave the other spreads untouched (the spreads opposite the side under duress). More aggressive traders will roll up those spreads behind the index price movement. This confirms the profit in those spreads and helps offset the losses from rolling the other side of the position. However, this exposes the trader to a whipsaw if the index price suddenly turns back. Manage the new spread positions according to your trading system rules. When rolling your put spreads upward, don't forget to cancel the old stop-loss order and enter a new one.

IRON CONDOR TRADING SYSTEMS

A trading system is simply the collection of rules and tactics you have developed to guide your trading. It will include your rules for entering and exiting the trade. A crucial portion of your trading system deals with risk management: stop-loss order placement, adjustment techniques, rules concerning closing the trade before expiration week, and so on. It is critically important that these rules are formally written down.

You are the best-qualified person to develop your trading system because you know yourself best. You can judge how much risk is tolerable and what simply feels comfortable for you. Always pay attention to your comfort level. When in doubt, be conservative.

I have developed the following four iron condor trading systems for your use as starting points for developing your personal trading system. But don't take these as gospel. Revise and supplement these systems to make them your own.

Your trading system should not be a static document. Review your trades each month and consider whether a new rule is needed or some of your criteria need adjustment. Continue to learn from the market and fine-tune your trading system.

Conservative Short-Term Iron Condor Trading System

1. Initiate the iron condor position on the RUT at 25 to 30 days to expiration.
2. Calculate one standard deviation (σ) based on the average ATM IV for RUT and the number of days to expiration.
3. Position the short options of the spreads at or just outside $\pm 1\sigma$ or $\Delta \cong 10$.
4. Pull up a one-minute chart of the RUT for today. If the current trend is upward, enter the put spread orders first; if the trend is downward, enter the call spread orders first. Enter the order at the midpoint of the bid/ask spread; if unfilled after two to three minutes, adjust the credit limit downward by $0.05; proceed in this way until the order is filled. Then enter the other spread order.
5. The trigger price for the stop-loss order is $10 above the short put option strike price. Enter this order with your broker as a contingent order that will close the put spreads automatically if the trigger price is reached.
6. Check the debit to close each spread every day. If the debit is greater than twice the original credit for that spread, close all of the spreads on this side of the iron condor.
7. After closing one side of the iron condor position, calculate 1σ based on the average ATM IV for RUT and the remaining days to expiration. As long as the remaining spreads are $\geq 2\sigma$ OTM, allow those spreads to expire worthless.
8. If the position is still open on the Friday before expiration week, calculate 1σ based on the average ATM IV for RUT and the remaining days

to expiration. If either spread is $< 2\sigma$ OTM, close those spreads. Allow the spreads to expire worthless if they are $> 2\sigma$ OTM.

Conservative Long-Term Iron Condor Trading System

1. Initiate the iron condor position on the RUT at 45 to 55 days to expiration.

2. Calculate one standard deviation (σ) based on the average ATM IV for RUT and the number of days to expiration.

3. Position the short options of the spreads one strike price beyond $\pm 1\sigma$ or $\Delta \cong 7$ to 10.

4. Pull up a one-minute chart of the RUT for today. If the current trend is upward, enter the put spread orders first; if the trend is downward, enter the call spread orders first. Enter the order at the midpoint of the bid/ask spread; if unfilled after two to three minutes, adjust the credit limit downward by $0.05; proceed in this way until the order is filled. Enter the other spread order.

5. Open the RUT option chain for the month you are trading. Identify the put option with a delta of 33 to 35. Take the difference between that strike price and the current RUT price and add that to the short put strike price in the position's put spreads. That is the trigger price for your stop-loss order. Enter this order with your broker as a contingent order that will close the put spreads automatically if the trigger price is reached.

6. Monitor the delta of the short options in each spread. If the delta of the short option ≥ 16, then buy the option at that strike price in the next month out in the options chain. Buy one option for every ten spreads in the position.

7. If the delta of the short option reaches or exceeds 25, close the spreads on that side of the position and sell the long hedge options.

8. After closing one side of the iron condor position, calculate 1σ based on the average ATM IV for RUT and the remaining days to expiration. As long as the remaining spreads are $\geq 2\sigma$ OTM, allow those spreads to expire worthless.

9. If the position is still open on the Friday before expiration week, calculate 1σ based on the average ATM IV for RUT and the remaining days to expiration. If either spread is $< 2\sigma$ OTM, close those spreads. Allow the spreads to expire worthless if they are $> 2\sigma$ OTM.

Aggressive Short-Term Iron Condor Trading System

1. Initiate the iron condor position on the RUT at 25 to 30 days to expiration.

2. Calculate one standard deviation (σ) based on the average ATM IV for RUT and the number of days to expiration.

3. Position the short options of the spreads inside $\pm 1\sigma$ or $\Delta \cong 22$ to 25.

4. Pull up a one-minute chart of the RUT for today. If the current trend is upward, enter the put spread orders first; if the trend is downward, enter the call spread orders first. Enter the order at the midpoint of the bid/ask spread; if unfilled after two to three minutes, adjust the credit limit downward by $0.05; proceed in this way until the order is filled. Enter the other spread order.

5. The trigger price for the stop-loss order is the short put option strike price. Enter this order with your broker as a contingent order that will close the put spreads automatically if the trigger price is reached.

6. Check the debit to close each spread every day. If the debit is greater than twice the original credit for that spread, close all of the spreads on this side of the iron condor.

7. After closing one side of the iron condor position, calculate 1σ based on the average ATM IV for RUT and the remaining days to expiration. As long as the remaining spreads are $\geq 2\sigma$ OTM, allow those spreads to expire worthless.

8. Monitor the position's overall net gain/loss daily. If the gain exceeds 25%, close half of the contracts.

9. On the Friday before expiration week, close the position.

Aggressive Long-Term Iron Condor Trading System

1. Initiate the iron condor position on the RUT at 45 to 55 days to expiration.

2. Calculate one standard deviation (σ) based on the average ATM IV for RUT and the number of days to expiration.

3. Position the short options of the spreads either at or just outside $\pm 1\sigma$ or $\Delta \cong 10$.

4. Pull up a one-minute chart of the RUT for today. If the current trend is upward, enter the put spread orders first; if the trend is downward, enter the call spread orders first. Enter the order at the midpoint of the

bid/ask spread; if unfilled after two to three minutes, adjust the credit limit downward by \$0.05; proceed in this way until the order is filled. Enter the other spread order.

5. Open the RUT options chain for the month you are trading. Identify the put option with a delta of 33 to 35. Take the difference between that strike price and the current RUT price and add that to the short put strike price in the position's put spreads. That is the trigger price for our stop-loss order. Enter this order with your broker as a contingent order that will close the put spreads automatically if the trigger price is reached.

6. Monitor the delta of the short options in each spread. If the delta of the short option ≥ 20, then buy the option at that strike price in the next month out in the options chain. Buy one option for every ten spreads in the position.

7. If the delta of the short option ≥ 30, close the spreads on that side of the position and sell the long hedge options.

8. If > 20 days remain to expiration, calculate 1σ based on the average ATM IV for RUT and the number of days to expiration. Establish new spreads to replace those just closed at $\pm 1\sigma$.

9. Close the spreads on the other side of the iron condor and roll them up or down to $\pm 1\sigma$ OTM. Manage the new iron condor position as in steps 6 and 7 above.

10. On the Friday before expiration week, calculate 1σ based on the average ATM IV for RUT and the remaining days to expiration. If either spread is < 2σ OTM, close those spreads. As long as the remaining spreads are $\geq 2\sigma$ OTM, allow those spreads to expire worthless.

BUTTERFLIES AND CONDORS ARE COUSINS

It will be helpful to your understanding of delta-neutral options trading to see the overall relationships between various options strategies. The condor spread can be considered as the logical extension of the butterfly spread. As soon as I pull apart the two sold options that form the body of the butterfly, my broker will margin the position as a condor, and the characteristics of the position begin to change.

In Figure 9.9, we have built an RUT iron butterfly as an example; we placed the long options at one standard deviation OTM and sold

Russell 2000 Index (RUT) = $668

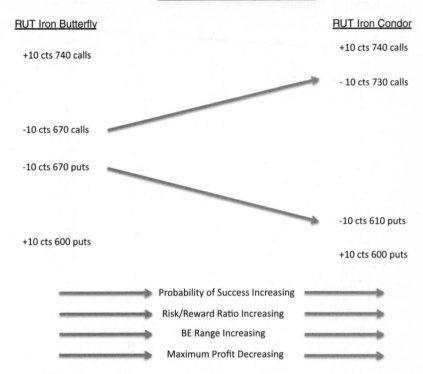

RUT Iron Butterfly

+10 cts 740 calls

-10 cts 670 calls

-10 cts 670 puts

+10 cts 600 puts

RUT Iron Condor

+10 cts 740 calls

- 10 cts 730 calls

-10 cts 610 puts

+10 cts 600 puts

Probability of Success Increasing

Risk/Reward Ratio Increasing

BE Range Increasing

Maximum Profit Decreasing

FIGURE 9.9   Butterflies and Condors Are Cousins

both of the ATM options. As we move the strike prices of the short options farther OTM, the risk/reward ratio shifts from closer to 1:1 to the higher risk/reward ratio typical of the iron condor—not good. However, the probability of success is increasing—good. And the break-even range is increasing—good. But the maximum profit available is decreasing—not good. We have trade-offs as we move from the iron butterfly to the iron condor.

This reinforces a foundational truth of options trading strategies. Each strategy has its own unique set of advantages and disadvantages. Each strategy has its own unique risk characteristics, and no single options strategy is the "best" strategy. There will always be trade-offs.

In the next chapter, we will summarize and contrast the characteristics of the delta-neutral options trading strategies we have discussed in the previous several chapters.

TABLE 9.5 February Options Chain for RUT on January 1, 2009

Calls			Puts	
Bid	Ask	Strike	Bid	Ask
117.90	121.50	$380	4.80	5.70
109.60	112.30	$390	6.00	6.70
100.90	103.70	$400	7.30	7.90
92.50	95.00	$410	8.80	9.50
84.30	86.70	$420	10.50	11.20
76.30	78.70	$430	12.50	13.40
68.70	71.10	$440	14.80	15.70
61.30	63.60	$450	17.50	18.50
54.30	56.50	$460	20.40	21.50
47.80	49.70	$470	23.70	24.90
41.60	43.30	$480	27.40	28.70
35.80	37.30	$490	31.60	32.90
30.50	31.90	$500	36.20	37.60
25.70	27.00	$510	41.30	42.80
21.50	22.60	$520	46.80	48.40
17.60	18.60	$530	52.80	54.50
14.30	15.10	$540	59.20	61.10
11.40	12.20	$550	66.10	68.20
8.90	9.70	$560	73.40	75.70
6.90	7.60	$570	81.30	83.60
5.20	5.90	$580	89.00	93.00
3.80	4.50	$590	97.70	101.60
2.70	3.50	$600	106.60	110.10
1.95	2.60	$610	115.50	119.50
1.05	1.95	$620	124.90	128.80
0.55	1.40	$630	134.40	138.40

EXERCISES

Refer to the options chain in Table 9.5 for all of the following questions. This is the actual data from January 1, 2009. RUT was trading at $499.45; IV = 48.63%, and the February options had 49 days to expiration.

1. Calculate one standard deviation. What are the closest strikes to $\pm 1\sigma$?

2. Using natural pricing (use the bid and ask), select the strikes for a Feb RUT iron condor at approximately $\pm 1\sigma$. Calculate the total credit received for 15 contracts. What is the maximum possible gain in dollars for this position? What is the maximum possible loss?

3. Move the strikes of the condor above farther ITM by one strike and recalculate.

4. What are the trade-offs between these two condors?

5. If you use $20 spreads for either of the preceding condors, what would you predict to change? Work through the calculations to confirm. Would you recommend this larger spread?

6. Consider the hypothetical situation with RUT trading at $500 and IV = 72%. IV has ranged from 25% to 72% over the past six months. A 2.5-point positive skew exists between the front month and the following month.

   a. Your friend, Bubba, proposes a $500 call calendar spread that promises a 32% maximum profit.

   b. Your friend with the funny accent, Arnold, proposes an iron condor with the strikes placed at $\pm 1.5\sigma$ and a 9% maximum return.

   c. Cite the advantages and disadvantages for each trade.

   d. Which trade would you place and why?

7. What is the most critical piece of advice you would give someone who is considering trading the iron condor spread? Why?

8. What is the principal advantage of the long hedge form of condor adjustment? What is its principal disadvantage?

9. What is the principal advantage of the 200% rule form of condor adjustment? What is its principal disadvantage?

10. What are the trade-offs between using the 200% rule and the long hedge forms of adjustment?

CHAPTER 10

Delta-Neutral Trading Strategies

W e have now explored in detail the principal delta-neutral trading strategies that may be used for consistent income generation: at-the-money (ATM) calendars, double calendars, double diagonals, ATM butterflies, ATM iron butterflies, condors, and iron condors. The individual risk characteristics of these strategies are summarized in Table 10.1.

Don't interpret the data of Table 10.1 too precisely; the objective of this table is to generalize among the delta-neutral trading strategies and make some broad comparisons and contrasts. Returns for these strategies vary considerably from condors and iron condors at the low end to butterflies and iron butterflies at the high end. However, any of these trades may be configured in such a way as to vary these values. For example, if we position the spreads of the iron condor much closer to the current value of the underlying index and initiate the trade with about 25 to 30 days to expiration, we have an iron condor with a much smaller risk/reward ratio and a much larger potential return than the standard long-term iron condor, positioned outside of one standard deviation with 50 days to expiration. But to a first approximation, butterflies will generally have higher potential returns and smaller risk/reward ratios than condors.

The calendars, double calendars and double diagonals are all large positive vega positions, although the vegas of the double diagonals are not quite as large as the calendars. If you believe decreasing volatility is likely, these are not the right trades for that market. For a similar reason, traders often use butterfly spreads to play stock price moves after earnings

TABLE 10.1   Characteristics of Delta-Neutral Trading Strategies

Strategy	Expected Return	Risk/ Reward	Break-even Range	Vega Risk	Complexity
ATM butterflies	High	Low	Broad	Low (−)	Low
ATM iron butterflies	High	Low	Broad	Low (−)	Low
ATM calendars	Mid	Mid	Broad	High (+)	Low
Double calendars	Mid	Mid	Broad	High (+)	Mid
Double diagonals	Low	High	Broad	Mid (+)	High
Condors	Low	High	Broad	Low (−)	High
Iron condors	Low	High	Broad	Low (−)	High

announcements because of their negative vegas. Implied volatility (IV) often crashes after the announcement, and that helps your butterfly spreads (as long as the price stays within your break-even range).

The complexity column of Table 10.1 is very subjective, and others may have a different view. I am including not only the complexity of establishing and managing the position, but also the required adjustments when the market moves against the position. Double diagonals, condors, and iron condors are all only moderately complex to establish and manage. However, long-term success with these strategies necessitates effective use of adjustment techniques. Choosing and appropriately deploying those adjustments increases the complexity of these strategies.

The strategies of Table 10.1 are known as delta-neutral strategies due to their minimal sensitivity to price changes in the underlying stock or index. Recall from Chapter 3 that the Greek delta (Δ) measures the sensitivity of our position to a change in the price of the underlying stock or index. Delta represents our risk due to a move in the price of the stock or index. When we establish a position with a small positive or a small negative delta, we have established a position with minimal risk resulting from a change in the underlying stock or index price. Thus, these are delta-neutral or price-neutral positions.

The basic strategy of the delta-neutral trade is to profit from time decay while the stock or index price trades within the break-even range of the position. The value of theta for these strategies will always begin as a positive value and increase in magnitude as the trade progresses and we near option expiration. This assumes the stock or index price does not trend strongly in one direction or the other. In real life, this assumption is frequently proven incorrect. In each of the chapters discussing these trading strategies, we have discussed in detail the variety of adjustment techniques available to manage the trade, maintain profitability, or at least minimize losses.

RISK MANAGEMENT SYSTEMS

Risk management is the most crucial aspect of any investment strategy, and this is equally true of options trading strategies. Many of the classic delta-neutral trading strategies have larger risk/reward ratios, necessitating a robust system of adjustments and stop losses to ensure that the trader never takes the large loss that is always possible, even though it may be a low-probability event. Just because the probability of the loss's occurring is low doesn't mean it won't happen to you! Successful delta-neutral traders begin with a well-defined trading system that includes a robust risk management system.

The phrase "robust risk management system" may connote a complicated array of interacting financial instruments with names like *subordinated debt swaps* and the like. However, effective risk management of the options strategies we have discussed in this book can be very straightforward. For each options trading strategy, the following aspects of risk management need to be in place:

- *Stop-loss.* This is the ultimate safety net for the trade. Many traders give lip service to the stop-loss and enter the trade by mentally noting a price where they will close the trade. This is the infamous *mental stop-loss.* It is infamous because it is so common for a position to get into trouble and be incurring large losses and the mental stop-loss has been forgotten; now the trader is focused on the different ways the markets may move to bail him out—the trader is now focused on hope. The stop-loss should always be entered with the broker as a contingent order to be triggered when a specific price of the underlying stock or index is reached. In that way, the trade is closed and a manageable loss has been incurred. This is actually a very healthy event for the trader's psyche. The trade is closed; he can move on and focus on the next opportunity.
- *Adjustment.* A wide variety of adjustment techniques are available to the trader, regardless of the options trading strategy. However, the effectiveness and advisability of various adjustments differ greatly. Sometimes closing the trade is the best "adjustment." We have discussed a variety of adjustments in each of the chapters discussing options trading strategies. Each adjustment technique has its own advantages and disadvantages. Options modeling software can be very helpful in these situations. The visual representation of a position's risk graph before and after the adjustment can be very enlightening. Options modeling also allows the trader to optimize the amount of the adjustment to be applied (e.g., should one or two contracts of long calls

be purchased?). Many adjustments require additional capital to be put at risk and this should be weighed carefully.

- *Profit stop.* The concept of a point in the trade where a large proportion of the potential profit has been achieved is important for the trader to consider in advance. This is similar to the psychological pitfalls associated with the mental stop-loss; when a trade is proceeding very well, it is easy to begin to focus on greater gains and end up giving back much of the profits as the market turns on us. Many delta-neutral trades have large potential gains that are not easily achieved in practice. For example, the butterfly spread has its peak profitability for the underlying stock or index price closing at expiration right at the short option strike price. But a much more reasonable profit can be estimated from the risk graph about ten days to expiration over a reasonably broad price range. Targeting a profit goal in advance and committing to close the trade when that profit level is reached is the profit stop.
- *Time stop.* Directional trades should have a point in time where the trader is willing to admit that his prediction didn't turn out as planned and he closes the trade. Nondirectional trades are somewhat different. The profit engine of the delta-neutral trade is time decay; as expiration approaches, the value of the credit spreads we sold declines, and we can buy those spreads back for a profit. A general rule for most delta-neutral strategies is to close the position on the Friday before expiration week. This is the time stop. Of course, one may have variations on that concept. For example, I normally carry my iron condor spread positions to that Friday and then make an evaluation. If either or both of the credit spreads are less than two standard deviations (2σ) OTM, I close those spreads. If the spreads are greater than 2σ OTM, I allow those options to expire worthless. This is another example of a time-stop rule, and some form of a time stop should be included in any trade system's risk management.

CHALLENGING MARKETS FOR THE DELTA-NEUTRAL TRADER

Strongly trending markets are difficult, but not impossible, challenges for delta-neutral trading strategies. The adjustments for each strategy are different but they rest on common principles. The adjustment accomplishes two purposes:

1. The adjustment contains losses in the main trade position (e.g., the iron condor) by initiating a position that profits as the market trend continues against our position.

2. The adjustment gives the trader time for the market to pull back. If it does pull back, the trader still has his position in place to generate a profit.

In strongly trending markets, the original portion of the trade that is under pressure may be closed at some point as the market continues to move against it. The trader then has the alternative of opening a new position to continue the trade. Often, the hedging position (the adjustment) is left open and continues to gain in profitability.

For these reasons, strongly trending markets can be handled by the delta-neutral trader when appropriate adjustments are made in a timely manner. The worst-case scenario should be a small loss or perhaps even a small gain.

Extremely volatile markets, with rapid swings both up and down, are the worst-case scenario for the delta-neutral trader. When the market trends strongly in one direction, the trader may employ various techniques to adjust the position and minimize the position's risk. In most cases, these adjustments will maintain profitability, albeit at a lower level. Thus, each adjustment costs the trader some of his potential profit—insurance costs money! In volatile markets, we may be forced to defend our put spreads in an iron condor position, for example, and then have the market turn around and run upward, forcing us to defend our call spreads. While we may be successful in avoiding the large loss for that trade, we may find ourselves in a position at some point with minimal or no potential profit left if the position is held to expiration. Losses in this situation may be exacerbated if the trader has rolled down the call spread positions behind the market's trend downward. If the market then swings back upward, the trader is scrambling to protect the call spread side of his trade, again reducing the potential profit of the trade.

A common mistake for beginning options traders is to assume that losses occur only when the trader makes a mistake. That isn't true. Losses are an expected cost of this business. Risk management minimizes those losses.

TWO DISTINCT TRADING PHILOSOPHIES

Two schools of thought exist for using delta-neutral trading strategies. The classic directional trader begins with a prediction for the direction and timing of the underlying stock or index price. That prediction may be based on an analysis of a company's business prospects or a technical analysis of the stock's price chart, or a combination of both. The result of the trader's analysis is a prediction for the price move of the stock or index and the timing of that move. Then he chooses the appropriate strategy to benefit from his prediction. Delta-neutral strategies may be used when a sideways price pattern for the stock or index is predicted. For the directional trader, the delta-neutral trade is simply one of many tools in the trader's toolbox to profit from his price and timing prediction.

The second school of thought for using delta-neutral trading strategies is fundamentally different. This trader is skeptical of his ability to predict the market's next move, so he wants a strategy that allows him to react to the market's price move and maintain a position that is relatively insensitive to changes in the price of the underlying stock or index. This allows the trade time to benefit from the time decay of the positive theta position. This nondirectional trader adjusts the position as necessary to maintain a relatively small risk due to price movement while maximizing theta decay.

The best analogy for the nondirectional trader's use of delta-neutral trading strategies is the insurance business. The premiums for auto insurance are based on statistical measures of risk for the driver (e.g., age, driving record, location, number of miles driven per year). Each delta-neutral trading strategy allows for some adjustment of the risk/reward ratio when establishing the trade. For example, when we establish the ATM butterfly spread and make the wings wider, we increase the break-even range, decrease the maximum profit, and increase the risk/reward ratio. Just as the insurance company collects a larger premium for the teenage driver to compensate for the higher statistical risk, we can position our delta-neutral trade to collect a higher potential profit, albeit with a correspondingly lower probability of success.

Insurance companies establish reserves to pay out on policies based on the statistical expectations of risk for the policyholders. The delta-neutral trader establishes a robust risk management system of adjustment techniques and stop losses that is similar to the insurance company reserve account in that it minimizes losses in the short term to maintain long-term profitability.

The insurance agent will sell you the auto insurance policy at any time. He may realize we are nearing winter weather and that a higher risk of accidents exists during the first few snowstorms. But that risk is built into the premium structure for policies issued in Chicago. In a similar way, the nondirectional delta-neutral trader is not required to predict market movement or volatility. Higher volatilities will result in higher option premiums, allowing the trader to either enjoy a higher potential return corresponding to the higher risk or move his spreads farther OTM and collect what he would consider his usual premium at his usual risk.

The nondirectional trader places his delta-neutral trades every month because he is not willing to predict future market movement; he doesn't know which months will be optimal for a delta-neutral trading strategy, so he trades every month just as the insurance agent sells policies every month. The delta-neutral trader simply responds to the current market price move without making a judgment about what might be coming tomorrow. That relieves the trader of the constant tension of wondering whether his prediction will be proven correct. He just calmly responds to the current market move with a predetermined plan for adjustment.

THE "SECRET" OF SUCCESS

All stock and options trading strategies share two critical success factors:

1. A systematic approach to establishing, managing, and closing the trade
2. Risk management

This systematic approach may also be called a trading system. It is the collection of rules and parameters used to enter, adjust, and exit the trade. One could argue that the trading system includes the risk management rules, and I would agree. However, I have separated risk management for emphasis.

These success factors are equally valid for the nondirectional delta-neutral trader. Delta-neutral trading strategies with larger risk/reward ratios must employ robust risk management for long-term success. Many losses occur because the trader begins to consider whether to adjust or which adjustment to employ only after the market has moved against his position. That is too late and allows the trader's emotions to cloud the thought process. Costly mistakes result.

Delta-neutral trading strategies also share a critical vulnerability. Rapidly trending markets and extreme market swings back and forth will devastate the profitability of delta-neutral trades. Fortunately, those market situations are unusual. Therefore, it is crucial that your trading system contains robust risk management to minimize losses during those extreme market conditions.

In the next chapter, we will address the critical steps to using one or more of these options trading strategies to build your trading system and transform your trading hobby into a business.

CHAPTER 11

Make Your Trading a Business

The vast majority of individual traders treat their trading like a hobby. They dabble in it when they have time. They trade tips from friends and acquaintances. They love to tell their friends about the big gain they made buying puts when Martha Stewart went to prison. But they don't have a trading system or a plan. No rules or techniques have been developed to manage the risk of the portfolio of trades. In fact, many of these traders like it just that way; they enjoy the excitement—they are gamblers.

Now is the time to ask yourself the hard question: Do I really want to make trading stocks and/or options a personal business, and perhaps even grow it to the point of supporting my family? If the answer is yes, then the rest of this chapter is devoted to the tools and ideas necessary to convert your trading from a hobby to a business.

GETTING STARTED

We all have a tendency to jump into any new activity wholeheartedly. In this instance of learning how to trade delta-neutral strategies, you will be best advised to jump into the study and paper trading of these strategies with as much time and energy as possible. However, take the actual live trading with real money much more slowly—and this advice is just as relevant for the student with $25,000 in his trading account as it is for the student with $500,000 in her trading account.

Trading options is not rocket science, but it is more nuanced than it might appear at first. Your learning curve will be reasonably long. One of the issues is simply the length of time for the typical delta-neutral trade. If I am playing long-term iron condors and I wish to manage only one position at a time, then I will have the experience of only three trades after six months of trading. I will gain experience faster if I am trading short-term iron condors, but even then, in the preceding scenario, I will have experience with only six trades after six months. You may find it difficult to be patient, but your patience will be rewarded.

Let's assume you have decided to trade at-the-money (ATM) iron butterflies as your delta-neutral strategy of choice. Each trade requires 20 to 30 days to play out. Thus, after six months, you have only six trades of experience. The essential profit generation engine of the delta-neutral trading strategy is time decay. Thus, delta-neutral trades take time to play out. In turn, this means your experience grows slowly.

Many novice traders have fallen into a common trap. Consider this hypothetical student: he opens his trading account with $100,000. He paper trades the short-term iron condor on SPX for two months and achieves paper profits both months. Then he opens a live trade with five contracts and makes a $1,100 profit the following month. Now he does a little calculation on the side and notes that if he had been trading 50 contracts last month, he could have pocketed $11,000. That gets him excited. So he jumps in with both feet and establishes a short-term iron condor with 50 contracts for the next month. But then the market moves down sharply; this trader's fear overwhelms him and he forgets all that he has learned about risk management and takes a $35,000 loss. The point of this anecdote is to patiently build your experience and scale up slowly.

Start your delta-neutral trading with only one or two contract positions. Trading commissions will take a disproportionate share of your profits until you reach ten contracts or more. These early trades are for learning, not making money. In these early stages, use the simplest trading plans we have reviewed as we explored each of the delta-neutral strategies. Either use the simplest adjustments, like the 200% rule for iron condors, or use no adjustments at all; simply employ rules to limit losses and to take profits. Many adjustment techniques aren't feasible for less than ten contracts.

As you gain experience and confidence, scale your position size slowly upward. When you begin to trade ten or more contracts, the other adjustment techniques may be feasible for risk management. Escalate slowly. If a trader is trading a large position that is new to him, he runs the risk of his emotions beginning to play a larger role. Emotions may cloud your vision and tempt you to deviate from your trading system and rules. Be sure your comfort level justifies scaling up to the next level. There is nothing wrong with proceeding slowly—it will save you money.

MANAGING LOSSES

Consider for a moment what characterizes effective business management. We could develop a long list, but controlling expenses would be near the top of everyone's list. There are several expenses associated with a trading business: computer hardware, software, Internet access, web site subscription fees, books, newsletters, and so on. But the most important expense is not listed here and may be easily overlooked: trading losses are the most important expense of your business that must be controlled and minimized. Risk management is the most critical factor determining your trading success. For that reason, I have emphasized risk management techniques for every trading strategy discussed in this book.

It is natural for human beings to look at activities with a positive expectation; we evaluate trading a butterfly spread with emphasis on the potential returns, not the potential losses. To make our trading business successful, we must focus on two concepts:

1. Losses are a natural and expected result of trading.
2. Trading losses must be carefully managed and controlled.

Realizing that losses are a normal part of trading is not easy to accept. Most of us have the capital necessary for trading because we have been successful in some other profession. And, most likely, we were not successful in that endeavor by being right 70% of the time. But the perfectionism that made us successful elsewhere can be our undoing in our trading business. I have emphasized risk management throughout this book. But the successful application of risk management techniques does not mean my account will never have a loss.

THE TRADING PLAN

Develop a written plan for each trading account that includes the following sections:

- Overall Purpose (e.g., retirement, monthly income, etc.)
- Return-on-Investment Goals (e.g., 18% annually or 2% monthly, etc.)
- Trading Strategies (e.g., ATM covered calls with blue-chip stocks)
- Trading Parameters (e.g., trade entry, stop-loss exit, profit exit, etc.)
- Risk Management (e.g., stop-loss rules, adjustment techniques, amount at risk on any one trade, etc.)

Establish a routine of reviewing all closed trades every month. Look for instances where you didn't follow your rules and resolve not to repeat that mistake. Look for areas where one of your rules needs to be adjusted or replaced with a different rule. It is especially important to distinguish "bad trades" from "losing trades." Both trades lost money, but the bad trade involved my breaking one or more of my rules. Losing trades are a normal part of this business; losing trades are a necessary cost of running this business.

Evaluating your closed trades every month is a valuable discipline that will improve your trading skills. However, beware of one common pitfall. It is easy to look at the price chart and postulate how much money I would have made if I had bought the option that day instead of the next day or whatever. If you followed your rules for entering the trade, then don't second-guess yourself. But if you see a pattern emerging over time, you may consider adjusting your trading rules accordingly. Some traders find themselves changing their trading systems so often that they effectively don't have a trading system. No trading system works 100% of the time.

MONEY MANAGEMENT

The term *money management* is used in different ways in the trading literature. I will use the term to refer to the allocation of capital to any one particular trade. The term *risk management* is the all-encompassing system of limiting risk that we have discussed throughout this book as we discussed the various options trading strategies. Risk management includes stop-loss orders, adjustment techniques, time stops, profit stops, and so on.

The maximum percentage of the trading account at risk on any one trade should be in the range of 1% to 5%. This is a personal risk tolerance choice, but I would recommend 1% to 2% maximum. Diligently following this rule will ensure that the trading account isn't wiped out or decimated by one trade that goes wrong. Risk capital is the lifeblood of your trading business.

Consider a trader who is trading a $50,000 account and is trading the covered call strategy. He has identified 2% of his trading account, or $1,000, as his maximum loss on any one position. He has identified IBM as one of his trade candidates for this month. IBM is trading at $129 and we plan to sell the $130 call for $3.00. His break-even is $126 and he decides to set his stop-loss to trigger at $125. Using the Black-Scholes pricing model, he calculates that if IBM dropped to $125 today, he could buy the $130 call back for about $1.50. If the stop-loss triggers, it will be sometime in the future, so this value of the $130 call is most likely higher than he would have to pay if he were stopped out of this trade. But he will use $1.50 as the worst-case scenario: he would lose $400 on the stock, spend $150 buying back the call, and he took in $300 when he sold the call; so his net loss if the stop-loss is triggered will be about $250. Therefore, he could buy as many as 400 shares of IBM for his covered call position because this position size would have a maximum loss of $1,000. Since he does not want to devote his entire account to the IBM trade, he establishes the covered call with 200 shares.

The trader then plans to buy the Apple Computer (AAPL) $220/$230 call spread for $5.65, with AAPL trading at $228. He sets his stop-loss to trigger when the credit to close the trade is $2.85 or less. This would result in a loss of $280 per contract. Therefore, no more than three contracts of this spread can be established within his money management rules.

Trading delta-neutral income strategies presents a different wrinkle to money management. Let's presume I have a $100,000 account that I want to use to trade iron condors for monthly income. I have decided to trade long-term iron condors, so I will have two positions on at any given time, one in the current month and one in the next month. I have decided to trade 40 contracts in each month, leaving extra capital in the account for trade adjustments. My average credit is $0.80 on a side, thus a maximum profit of $6,400 for 40 contracts, or a 19% return. My adjustment techniques will limit my losses in the bad months to $6,000 or less. This is the critical assumption; if my experience cannot support the contention that losses can be limited to $6,000 or less, then I need to severely limit the number of contracts in play to a lower number until I can confidently assess the maximum risk. And I may even limit the number of contracts because the $6,000 loss represents 6% of my account, a maximum loss on the high side of good money management guidelines. For this reason, I always instruct my students to begin trading delta-neutral strategies with a small number of contracts and scale up very slowly as their experience and confidence grows.

Following a strict regimen for money management will limit the losses on any one trade to a small percentage of the trading account.

THE PSYCHOLOGY OF TRADING

Perhaps the most critical characteristic shared by successful traders is their psychological approach to the market. All forms of financial investments have foundational knowledge that is essential to success in that market. I am not suggesting that you can simply think the right way and trade stocks, commodities, or any other market successfully. But you could be the world's foremost expert on the commodities market and still not be able to translate that knowledge into monetary success.

Two emotions, fear and greed, can be lethal to your financial success. Developing an unemotional, systematic approach to your trading and investments is crucial for success. The following ideas will help you control your emotions and improve your trading results.

Have a Written Plan for Every Trade

Before you buy that stock, option spread, or other investment, you must make some critical decisions. Write down your answers to the following questions: Why do I think this is a good idea? At what price will I admit that my idea is not working and close the trade? If appropriate for this trade, at what price will I make some adjustments to the position? At what price will I take my profits? The answers to these questions and others constitute your trading plan. Be sure you have a plan *before* you establish the trade.

Follow Your Plan

This may be the hardest aspect of trading you must master. Once you have your plan, you must have the discipline to follow the plan unemotionally. Don't allow yourself to rationalize how the stock is going to rebound or allow your ego to refuse to admit the mistake. When the stock price dips below your stop-loss price, close the position.

Don't hope. Don't rationalize. Follow your plan.

Evaluate Your Results

Develop a routine of reviewing your trading results periodically. As discussed earlier, distinguish between the "losing trades" and the "bad trades." Bad trades result when I break my own rules for entering the trade or lack the discipline to follow the plan. Losing trades are those where I followed all of my rules, but the trade just didn't work out as planned. These losses are simply a "cost of doing business." In any business, there are necessary expenses to keep the business open. Trading losses are an expected, necessary part of any investment activity. Developing a trading system and following the individual trade plans ensure that your profitable trades will outweigh your losses.

This Isn't Gambling

A common misperception holds that investing is akin to gambling. In fact, when you closely analyze the actual trades of many investors, they are indeed gamblers. They are following tips and hunches, investing large amounts on expected turnarounds, anticipating mergers, betting on start-ups, and so on. But consider the business of gambling—not the gambler, but the casino. The casino establishes a game where the casino holds a statistical edge; depending on the game, that edge may be rather small, of the order of 1% to 2%. The casino owner knows that one of his customers is a big winner today at one of the tables, but that doesn't concern him because he knows he has an edge. When averaged over all of the different players and games, and over the long term, the casino will come out ahead.

When you work hard to develop the knowledge of the market you are trading, develop a trading system, have a written plan for every trade, follow your plan with great discipline, and learn from your mistakes, you have positioned yourself as the casino owner, not one of the customers.

LIVING WITH THE TWO-HEADED MONSTER

We have discussed both directional options strategies and delta-neutral, or nondirectional, strategies in this book. When trading your prediction for a stock or index price move, you have many technical and fundamental analysis tools at your disposal. But trading a delta-neutral strategy is fundamentally different—a prediction of market price or direction isn't required. For example, I may position my iron condor on the Standard & Poor's 500 Index (SPX) based on a probability calculation and then proceed to adjust the position to keep it close to delta-neutral as time passes and the market moves up or down. With this strategy, I am responding to the market's price moves according to the rules of my trading system. I am not trying to predict the market's next move. In fact, managing my position on the basis of my market prediction may actually get me into trouble as I don't adjust my position because I am convinced the market is going to pull back.

But one can't run a trading business without an interest in the market and the variety of forces underlying its moves. This is what I am referring to as the *two-headed monster.* One of my heads is monitoring the position and constantly referring back to my trading system rules and deciding what actions, if any, are required based only on the market price at this moment and my rules. The other head is looking at support and resistance, predicting a move after the upcoming Federal Open Market Committee (FOMC) announcement, watching trading volume, moving averages, Bollinger bands, moving average convergence/divergence (MACD), and perhaps many other indicators. This part of my mind is trying its best to make sense out of the myriad bits of information and predict the future.

Success in trading requires both of these viewpoints to be active. For one thing, it would be unusual for a delta-neutral trader to never have any directional trades ongoing. But I would also argue that the delta-neutral trader may be well advised to shade some of his rules from time to time based on his market assessment. This may be as simple as establishing the iron condor with a little more safety margin to the downside, so we initiate the trade with the put spreads one or two strikes lower to result in a position delta of −25 instead of a delta closer to zero.

So learn to live with the two-headed monster and benefit from directional insights and predictions when appropriate, but don't pervert your delta-neutral strategies into directional, speculative strategies.

REQUIRED TOOLS FOR THIS BUSINESS

Options Analysis Software

The web site platforms for the major options brokerages have grown markedly in sophistication over the past several years. So your broker's trading platform most likely has at least a rudimentary version of an options analysis program; several are quite sophisticated. Throughout this book, you have seen examples of the risk/reward graphs plotted from the Platinum software from Optionetics. Similar programs are available from other vendors as well as some of the options brokers. Options analysis software is essential for trading options and should offer the following capabilities:

- Plots risk/reward graphs at expiration and at different time intervals before expiration.
- Enables "what-if" analyses; for example, one may try out different adjustments for a trade and see the effects on the risk/reward graphs and the position Greeks.
- Enables backtesting. This is essential for analyzing closed trades to see if different trading system rules would have worked better. This is also useful for trying out a new strategy or a new set of trading rules.
- Plots new risk/reward graphs for changes in implied volatility (IV). IV changes are one of the critical risk factors for your options position; this is an important "what-if" analysis.
- Includes search tools to scan the stocks and options universe for candidates for a particular strategy; for example, we may be searching for overvalued options for selling covered calls or naked puts.
- Maintains a database of current and past trades to enable retrospective analysis of individual trades and portfolio profit-and-loss analysis.

Telecommunications

High-speed Internet access is essential for your trading business. The choices available to you vary by location, but my recommendation is to purchase the fastest service available to you. You don't want to be waiting several seconds for a screen to refresh when the market is moving against your position. If power outages occur even infrequently in your area, you might consider having a laptop with wireless capability available; in the event of an outage, you can seek out the nearest coffee shop with free wireless Internet access and continue to monitor your positions.

Computing Hardware

It is probably self-evident that a personal computer is required for trading in today's markets. The days of picking up the phone to place a stock or options order are gone. The PC and Mac wars continue, but my personal choice has always been the Mac. I have found it much easier to use, and the current Mac operating system is far more dependable and secure. The movement in recent years to web-based applications has made the Mac a more viable choice for trading online, even though the finance professionals in the exchanges are still tied to the Windows operating system.

The stereotypical picture of the trader includes a workstation with several computer display screens on the desk or hanging on the wall. If you are a day trader who follows many different markets and watches the market in different timeframes (minute, daily, and weekly charts), then those multiple screens may be necessary. The modern liquid crystal display (LCD) screens are large enough to have at least two windows open and visible simultaneously, so I don't believe multiple monitors are necessary for trading the strategies we have discussed in this book. I have a 30-inch LCD display that enables me to easily write this chapter in Word while having my brokerage account window open and displaying real-time quotes.

WHAT'S NEXT?

Trading delta-neutral options strategies is a very powerful tool for generating a steady income from your accounts. Much of the marketing for courses and other services in this business portrays this as easy and fast. Hopefully, this book has served to put this subject in a more realistic light.

Yes, it is feasible.

You don't have to be a rocket scientist.

You don't have to know "the secret."

But it does require knowledge and hard work.

And it will not happen overnight.

My students often ask me how long it will take for them to become proficient options traders. There isn't any one answer. Each person has different abilities. But more importantly, each person approaches the subject in his or her own way. Some devote many hours in the evenings and weekends and come up to speed much faster. But the most important teacher is experience, and that takes time. Most students will feel some success and gain a measure of confidence after about six months of trading, but they will also realize they are still learning and that process will continue. I am still learning new things about the market, and the market itself is changing, so the learning process never ends.

I strongly recommend that you find yourself a trading coach or mentor. Check out the services offered at my web site, www.Parkwood CapitalLLC.com. There are many good coaches in this business, but unfortunately, there are also many people promoting unrealistic "get-rich-quick" schemes. Study the coach or educator's web site in advance, and then discuss your situation and goals with the prospective coach and watch for some critical warning signs:

- You are directed to a salesperson rather than the coach himself or herself.
- You are told this is easy; anyone can do it.
- The prospect of quitting your day job is dangled as an enticement.
- Examples of 100% gains or more are cited as possibilities.
- The learning curve is described in terms of weeks rather than months and years.

If any of these warning signs appear, don't consider this person or company further.

Finding a trading group that meets regularly is also a good idea for continuing your education. But be sure the group is led by someone with solid credentials and experience. Too often, trading groups are amateurs sharing ignorance and perpetuating some of the trading myths.

To continue and deepen your education on options trading, I recommend two excellent books:

Lawrence McMillan, *Options as a Strategic Investment*, 4th edition (Paramus, NJ: New York Institute of Finance, 2002). Order the accompanying study guide as well.
Sheldon Natenberg, *Option Volatility and Pricing* (New York: McGraw-Hill, 1994).

Of course, there are many excellent books and DVDs on options trading, but these two books are the ones I find myself referring back to time and time again.

No one is more interested in your financial future than you. So it behooves you to invest time and energy into managing your own finances. At a minimum, you should learn enough to know what your financial adviser is doing on your behalf. As you embark on this journey to become an options trader, remember the basics:

- Always trade with a written plan.
- Clearly specify the risk management techniques in the plan.
- Control your emotions and follow your plan with great discipline.

If you have read this far, drop me a note via the Contact Us screen on my web site, www.ParkwoodCapitalLLC.com. You are eligible for a free month's membership in Dr. Duke's Trading Group and the *Flying with the Condor*™ trading advisory service.

Good luck and best wishes for your journey in trading.

Answers to the Chapter Exercises

H ere are the answers to the exercises you read at the end of certain chapters. The exercise questions are repeated here for your convenience.

CHAPTER 2

1. GOOG closed today at $353.02 with only one day left in October's options. Implied volatility of the Oct $350 call option is 241%. GOOG will announce earnings after the close.

   a. Calculate the probability of the Oct $350 call expiring ITM (i.e., with the stock price > $350).

   53%

   b. Assume you are very bullish on GOOG; what is the probability of GOOG's closing by expiration above $400?

   16%

   c. We would have to pay $7 or $700 for one contract of the Oct $400 calls. What will these calls be worth on expiration Friday (tomorrow) if GOOG closes at $408?

   This option will open a little over $8 and decline through the day to $8 as time value decays.

   d. Why is the implied volatility so high?

   The upcoming earnings announcement after the close.

    e. True or false: This extremely high IV means the market thinks GOOG is going much higher.

       False. High IV implies a wide swing in price is expected, but that swing could be up or down.

    f. What price range for GOOG would you predict for tomorrow with a 68% probability?

       The current price of $353 ± 1σ = $44.5 or $309 to $398.

2. IBM is trading at $91.52, IV = 63%, and Nov options have 36 days to expiration. We buy a $70/$80 bull call spread for $8.80. Our maximum profit of $1.20 will occur if IBM closes on expiration Friday above $80. Our maximum loss of $8.80 will occur if IBM closes on expiration Friday below $70.

    a. What is the probability of success for this trade?

       75%

    b. What is the probability of the maximum loss occurring?

       9%

    c. If you were to place a trade similar to this on IBM every month for a year, how many months would you predict you would be successful?

       About 9 months out of the year (75% of 12 months).

    d. Would you expect to be profitable at the end of the year? Why or why not?

       The risk-adjusted return = (0.75 × $120) − (0.09 × $880) = $11 or essentially break-even or a loss after commissions.

3. XOM is trading at $69.45, IV = 83%, and Nov options have 36 days to expiration. We buy a $80/$90 bull call spread for $1.57. Our maximum profit of $8.43 will occur if XOM closes on expiration Friday above $90. Our maximum loss of $1.57 will occur if XOM closes on expiration Friday below $80.

    a. What is the probability of success for this trade?

       16%

    b. What is the probability of a maximum loss occurring?

       71%

    c. If you were to place a trade similar to this on XOM every month for a year, how many months would you predict you would be successful?

       About 16% of the time or two months out of the year.

4. Compare and contrast the IBM and XOM trades in questions 2 and 3. Which trade is best? Why?

    Neither trade is "best." Over time, you would expect both strategies to approximately break even (absent some type of risk management to control the losses).

5. One of your friends tells you he is trading a very conservative options strategy that has a 90% probability of success, so he has cashed in his entire stock portfolio to invest in this strategy because he "can't lose." Without even knowing the details of the options strategy, what can you tell your friend about the likely outcomes of this strategy over time?

    It appears to be a high-probability trade, and this type of trade has a large risk/reward ratio; thus, it will be characterized by frequent small gains and infrequent large losses. The pattern will be such that the losses will overwhelm the gains in time (absent some type of risk management to control the losses). You should warn your friend that the losses for this strategy have a low probability of occurrence, but when the loss occurs, it will be large.

6. We are considering three trades:

    (1) IBM is trading at $118, IV = 23%, and we have 46 days to expiration of the October options. We are considering a spread where IBM must close above $130 at expiration to make 400% on the trade.

    (2) BAC is trading at $18, IV = 49%, and we have 46 days to expiration of the October options. We are considering a spread where BAC must close above $25 at expiration to make 1,037% on the trade.

    (3) AIG is trading at $45, IV = 152%, and we have 46 days to expiration of the October options. We are considering a spread where AIG must close above $55 at expiration to make 213% on the trade.

    a. Compute the expected return for each proposed trade.

    IBM: 0.12 × 400% = 48%
    BAC: 0.029 × 1037% = 30%
    AIG: 0.36 × 213% = 77%

    b. Which trade would you consider best and why?

    The AIG trade has the highest risk-adjusted return (or expected return), but it is a high-risk trade because of the very high IV. This volatility is accounted for in the expected return, but a conservative trader may be more comfortable with the IBM trade with a reasonable return with lower volatility.

CHAPTER 3

1. What do we normally use the Black-Scholes equation to calculate?

   The Black Scholes equation is used to calculate the theoretical price for an option given a specific stock price, the strike price of the option, the value of historical volatility, interest rate, and the time left to expiration.

2. Explain the difference between historical volatility and implied volatility.

   Historical volatility is the actual recorded price volatility of the stock over a specific period of time. Implied volatility is the market's prediction of future volatility; it is the volatility that is implied by the option's market price being either higher or lower than the theoretical value.

3. If the Market Volatility Index (VIX) is higher than it has been in the last 12 months, what does that tell me?

   The market as a whole is expecting broad market volatility to be larger in the next 30 days. But a higher VIX has no predictive value for future market direction.

4. An option's price has three components. Name them and explain how they fluctuate in the market.

   An option's market price is composed of three quantities: intrinsic or real value, time to expiration, and implied volatility. Intrinsic value is determined by how far in-the-money (ITM) the option is; options that are farther ITM have higher values. Options with more time to expiration and higher levels of implied volatility have higher prices.

5. Define the Greeks: delta, gamma, vega, and theta.

   Delta tells us how much the option will gain or lose in value with a $1 change in the price of the stock. Gamma measures the change in value of delta with a $1 change in the price of the stock. Vega measures the change in the value of the option with a 1% change in implied volatility. Theta measures the change in the option value with the passage of one day of time. All of these Greeks assume that all other variables are held constant; that is, the value of vega assumes that the stock price and time to expiration remain fixed while the implied volatility increases by one percent.

6. What does it mean if my position delta is +$105?

If the price of the underlying stock rises by $1, my position will gain $105 in value, or if the stock price decreases by $1, my position will lose $105.

7. If implied volatility is at historically high levels, would I want my position vega to be positive or negative? Why?

   Negative, because a drop in IV is more likely if IV is at record high levels. When IV drops with a negative vega position, the position gains in value.

8. When is theta positive and when is it negative?

   Theta is negative when I am long options and positive when I am short options. When I own spreads so that I am both long and short options, theta for the position may be positive or negative; it is the sum of the thetas for the individual options.

9. If I own an ATM call option and the underlying stock price and implied volatility remain unchanged, will my position's value be increased, decreased, or unchanged? Why?

   The call option will decrease in value due to the loss of time value or theta decay.

CHAPTER 4

1. In general terms, how do I establish an options spread?

   Buy one option and sell another option; vertical spreads are created by buying one option and moving up or down one or more strike prices in the same expiration month and selling that option.

2. Where do vertical spreads get their name?

   When option prices were displayed on the wall of the exchange originally, the prices were arranged in columns for each expiration month; each horizontal row was for a single strike price. Buying and selling options in the same expiration month was from the same vertical column on the board, hence, a vertical spread.

3. If I am bullish on IBM at today's price, what two different types of vertical spreads could I establish? Compute the maximum profit, maximum loss, and break-even of each spread.

   There are several possible answers; be sure you understand how to calculate the maximum gain and maximum loss for each type of spread. With IBM = $129, the 120/130 bull call spread is established with a debit of $710 (maximum loss); the maximum *profit will be $1,000 − $710 = $290 or 41%. The 120/130 put spread could be established for a credit of $310 (maximum profit of 45%); the maximum loss would be $1,000 − $310 = $690.*

4. What are the margin requirements for the two spreads in question 3?

   The $10 credit spread has a margin requirement of $1,000 per contract; the debit spread has no margin requirement.

5. Which of the two spreads in question 3 is the better choice? Why?

   The returns for credit and debit spreads at the same strikes will always be very close, if not identical; the preference is one of personal style.

6. If I were bullish on IBM at $118, what would be an example of an aggressive bullish spread versus a conservative bullish spread?

   A conservative spread would be an ITM spread like the $90/ $100 debit call spread; an aggressive spread would be the OTM spread, like the $120/$130 debit call spread.

7. I buy a GOOG $490/$500 call spread for $450 just a few days before the earnings announcement and IV is at record high levels. IV collapses after the announcement and two weeks later both options expire ITM. What profit, if any, did I make? What effect did the change in IV have on my position?

   Since both options expired ITM, the spread is worth $1,000 at expiration; since it was purchased for $450, the profit was $550. The collapse in IV would have made it easier to close the spread early for a large proportion of the profit, but it had no effect on the profit at expiration.

8. I was bearish on IBM when it was trading at $113, and I sold the $115/$110 call spread. Several weeks later, IBM is trading for $98 and I want to close the position. What orders would you place to close the spread?

   Buy to close (BTC) the $110 call, and sell to close (STC) the $115 call for a net debit.

9. The IBM position in question 8 can be closed with one order or two separate orders. What are the pros and cons of the two approaches?

   The differences are minor, but often a better price can be negotiated for two individual option orders than for a spread.

10. My account balance is $25,200. I sell 20 GOOG $510/$520 call spreads for $534/contract. What is my account balance after placing this trade? How much margin will be required?

Selling the spreads brings in 534 × 20 = $10,680. The account balance will be $35,880; $20,000 of margin will be required for 20 contracts of a $10 spread.

11. As I approach expiration Friday with the GOOG spread above, GOOG is trading at $510. What choices do you have? What would you recommend?

    You can allow the spread to go into expiration and settle, or you can buy it back to close it out before expiration. It would be best to close the spread for a profit before expiration. A minor price change near the close could result in GOOG's closing at a price above $510; then the $520 calls would expire worthless, and the $510 calls would be exercised against you, forcing you to sell short 2,000 shares of GOOG at $510 for a total of $1,020,000—probably not what you want.

12. I own 15 IBM $100/$110 call spreads. We are three days from expiration and IBM is trading at $123. Is early exercise of the short $110 calls likely? What would you do?

    Early exercise is possible but not likely unless we are near an ex-dividend date. In any case, you are indifferent to the exercise because the broker will exercise your $100 calls to satisfy the exercise, leaving you with your full $1,000 credit for each contract exercised. Allow the spreads to be automatically exercised at expiration.

CHAPTER 5

1. Why is the covered call "covered" and a naked put position "uncovered" or "naked"?

    When the call is exercised against us in the covered call trade, we already own the stock that is required to be sold, so we are "covered." If the put I have sold is exercised against me, I must purchase the shares of stock; the only way I can be covered is to have a short stock position in my account. So normally I am not covered, or "naked," for the exercise.

2. How could you use the selling naked puts strategy?

    Selling naked puts can be used for income generation or accumulating stock at a discount.

3. True or false: the covered call strategy is more conservative than the selling naked puts strategy. Why or why not?

False. Both positions have identical risk/reward profiles.

4. Compare and contrast the expected returns for the covered call strategy vs. the selling naked puts strategy.

   If one trades naked puts on a fully cash-secured basis, the returns are very similar to covered calls. If one trades the naked puts strategy on margin, the returns will be substantially larger but more risk is incurred.

5. Assume the naked puts margin requirement for your broker is 25% for the following questions:

   a. Assume AAPL is trading at $182. If my expectation for AAPL were slightly bullish, which put would you sell? If we sold the $185 put for $8.30, what is the maximum return on ten contracts? Under what circumstances will we achieve that return?

   Sell the $185 put if you expect AAPL to trade above $185; 25% of the amount we would pay if the puts were exercised against us is 0.25 × $185,000 = $46,250; 18% return (8300/46250) would be achieved if AAPL closes at expiration above $185.

   b. If the above trade were placed in my IRA account, what would the maximum return be?

   The broker will require a put sale in an IRA account to be fully cash secured; that means we have $185,000 as a margin requirement; therefore, the return is 4.5% (8,300/185,000).

6. Assume I sold ten contracts of the Sept $170 AAPL put for $5.60 a couple of weeks ago. As I approach September expiration, AAPL is trading at $182 and the Sept $170 put is trading at $0.05 × $0.07. What should I do and why?

   Buying back the Sept $170 put to close the position is the best approach; one could argue that AAPL's price is $12 above the strike price and that should be safe, but you would be exposed to any last-minute price changes—unlikely, but a problem if it happens.

7. I have an account with a $50,000 balance. Earlier, I sold five contracts of the Sept $480 puts for GOOG. As we near expiration, GOOG is trading at $488. What should I do and why?

   Buy back the puts; your account does not have nearly enough cash to accept the exercise if it were to happen. That would require $240,000.

8. I sold one contract of the Sept $180 puts for AAPL. On expiration Friday, AAPL closes at $188. What will happen? If AAPL had closed at $179, what would have happened?

> *At $188, the $180 puts expire worthless. At $179 those puts will be exercised against you, requiring you to buy 100 shares of AAPL at $180.*

9. What safeguards should I employ when selling naked puts?

   Always have a stop-loss order entered to execute automatically in the event the stock price drops unexpectedly.

10. Develop covered call scenarios for RIMM (trading at $82) and selling the $85 call at $5.50, and for GOOG (trading at $488) and selling the $490 call at $15.80. Assume you have a $50,000 account and all positions are called away at expiration.

    a. Work out the potential returns for investing all of your account in a covered call trade for (1) RIMM and (2) GOOG.

    b. Why are the results so different?

    > *I can afford to buy 600 shares of RIMM and sell the calls; the called-out return would be 11% ($1,800 from price appreciation and $3,300 from selling the calls; net investment is $47,700).*

    > *I can afford to buy 100 shares of GOOG and sell the calls; the called-out return would be 3.8% ($200 from price appreciation and $1,580 from selling the calls; net investment is $47,220).*

    > *The primary difference is the high share price of GOOG that required us to make a much larger investment; we could only buy 100 shares. Thus, our income was based on a larger investment and the return was smaller.*

CHAPTER 6

1. Name the two principal risk factors for double calendar spreads.

   A decrease in implied volatility and changes in the underlying stock or index price.

2. What is the advantage of a double calendar over an ATM calendar?

   The position will be profitable over a wider range of price.

3. When would you use an OTM call calendar instead of a double calendar?

   The OTM call calendar would be used when we expect the price of the underlying stock to rise.

4. I have chosen the strikes for my double calendar and the position delta is –$50. What does this tell you about my prediction for this stock?

This position is leaning bearish; that is, we have room for the stock price to move downward and the trade will become more delta-neutral. Apparently, I have some concerns that the stock may decline so I have given myself some safety margin to the downside.

5. I have a Jan/Apr $200 call calendar on AAPL. As we approach January expiration, AAPL is trading at $198. What are your choices?

   (1) Close the position for a profit.
   (2) Buy back the Jan $200 call and sell the Feb $200 call.

6. If I am considering different strike prices for a double calendar on the Russell 2000 Index (RUT), what will change if I move the strikes closer together?

   The break-even range will decrease; the potential return and the debit to establish the trade will both increase.

7. We established a Nov/Dec 110/130 double calendar on IBM with 30 days left in Nov and IBM was trading at $120. IBM trades up to $130 over the next ten days. What should I do?

   Close half of the $130 call calendars and open an equal number of $140 call calendars. Close all of the $110 put calendars and open an equal number of $120 put calendars.

CHAPTER 7

Consult the options chains in Tables 7.1 and 7.2 for the following exercises.

1. Assume we just purchased five AAPL Jan 2011 $180 calls for $39.80. AAPL closed today at $193. We have 12 days left in December and 40 days in January. Consult the options tables and decide:

   a. Which option will you sell? Why did you choose that one?

   Several answers are possible, depending on your prediction for AAPL. If not very bullish on AAPL, sell the $190 strike; if more bullish, sell the $195 call or the $200 call.

   b. What is your cost basis in your LEAPS calls?

   If I sold the Dec $200 call at $2.17, cost basis = $37.63.

   c. Assume we decided to sell the Dec $190 call for $6.55. What is our cost basis in the Jan 2011 $180 calls?

   $39.80 − $6.55 = $33.25

TABLE 7.1	AAPL December 2009 Options Chain

AAPL Dec 2009 Calls			AAPL Dec 2009 Puts		
Strike	Bid	Ask	Strike	Bid	Ask
170	23.55	23.70	170	0.25	0.28
175	18.75	18.90	175	0.46	0.48
180	14.20	14.35	180	0.87	0.92
185	10.05	10.15	185	1.71	1.75
190	6.55	6.65	190	3.15	3.20
195	3.90	3.95	195	5.50	5.60
200	2.17	2.18	200	8.75	8.85
210	0.56	0.57	210	17.05	17.25

d. As we approach Dec expiration, AAPL is trading at $190.52. What should you do?

Roll out to Jan $190 by buying back the Dec $190 call and selling the Jan $190 call.

e. As we approach Dec expiration, AAPL is trading at $188.21. What should you do?

Same answer as above; you don't want to risk this option expiring ITM. The broker will exercise your LEAPS to satisfy the exercise of the $190 calls and you will lose all of the time value in the LEAPS (almost $10,000).

f. As we approach Dec expiration, AAPL is trading at 201.10. What should you do?

TABLE 7.2	AAPL January 2010 Options Chain

AAPL Jan 2010 Calls			AAPL Jan 2010 Puts		
Strike	Bid	Ask	Strike	Bid	Ask
170	25.25	25.45	170	1.86	1.92
175	21.05	21.25	175	2.66	2.72
180	17.15	17.35	180	3.75	3.85
185	13.65	13.80	185	5.20	5.35
190	10.60	10.70	190	7.05	7.25
195	8.00	8.10	195	9.50	9.60
200	5.85	5.95	200	12.35	12.50
210	2.98	3.05	210	19.40	19.55

Roll to Jan $190 calls. If the credit to roll is less than $1, then close the trade. If bullish on AAPL, roll to Jan $200 for a debit.

2. Assume we purchased three Jan 2011 $180 calls for $39.80. We sold three Dec $190 calls for $6.55, and they expired worthless. We then sold the Jan $190 calls for $4.25. As we near Jan expiration, AAPL is trading at $195. We roll our Jan $190 calls to Feb $190 for a net credit of $3.76. If our Feb calls expire worthless and the Jan 2011 $180 calls are sold at $35.83, what is our return?

$39.80 − $6.55 = $33.25 initial cost basis
$33.25 − $4.25 − $3.76 = $25.24 final cost basis
Profit = $35.83 − $25.24 = $10.59 or $1,059/contract or $3,177
Original investment = $33.25 × 3 contracts = $9,975, so we had a 32% return.

3. As we approach Feb expiration, we are short the AAPL Feb $190 calls and long the AAPL 2011 $180 calls. AAPL has an earnings announcement tomorrow and you are bullish on AAPL. What should you do?

Buy back the Feb calls and hold the LEAPS.

4. We wish to establish the Dec/Jan AAPL 170/180 put and 200/210 call double diagonal.

   a. What will it cost to establish ten contracts of this position?

   Buy the Jan 210 call for $305 and sell the Dec $200 call for $217 for a net debit of $88.
   Buy the Jan $170 put for $192 and sell the Dec $180 put for $87 for a net debit of $105.
   Total debit for ten contracts is $1,930.

   b. If AAPL trades above the upper break-even after ten days in the trade, what adjustment options are open to you?

   Create a double calendar by buying the Jan $200 call and selling the Dec $210 call, or create a calendar spread by buying back the Dec $200 call and selling the Dec $210 call.

   c. If AAPL closes at $195 at Dec expiration, and the Dec options expire worthless, describe two alternatives you have facing you. Which would you choose and why?

   You can either close the trade by selling the Jan options, or establish an iron condor in January with the remaining options by selling the Jan $200 calls and selling the Jan $180 puts. In this case, I would close the trade since AAPL's price is too close to $200 to establish a condor spread.

CHAPTER 8

1. On January 28, 2009, GOOG closed at $349. A trader is considering the following spreads:
   a. Jan 2010 400/450/500 call butterfly
   b. Mar 330/350/370 call butterfly
   c. Mar 300/320/340 put butterfly

   What would you infer was the trader's expectation for GOOG if he were to establish each of these trades?

   a. The Jan 2010 butterfly expects GOOG to trade into the rough range of about $430 to $470 by January expiration—very bullish.
   b. The March call butterfly presumes GOOG will trade sideways for the next couple of months.
   c. The March put butterfly is based on a prediction for GOOG to trade down to about $320.

2. Based on the Jan 2010 options chain in Table 8.1 below, compute the initial credit or debit and the margin requirement for each of the following RUT spreads with RUT at $598:
   a. Jan 570/600/630 call butterfly
   $780 debit; no margin requirement.
   b. Jan 570/600/630 iron butterfly
   $2,220 credit; $3,000 margin requirement; some brokers may charge for both sides or $6,000.

TABLE 8.1 RUT January 2010 Options Chain

Jan 2010 Calls			Jan 2010 Puts	
Bid	Ask	Strike Price	Bid	Ask
54.70	55.60	550	8.30	8.70
46.50	47.30	560	10.20	10.50
39.10	39.70	570	12.70	13.10
32.10	32.60	580	15.60	16.00
25.70	26.20	590	19.10	19.50
20.00	20.40	600	23.40	23.90
15.10	15.50	610	28.40	29.00
11.00	11.30	620	34.30	34.90
7.70	8.10	630	41.00	41.70

    c. Jan 570/600/630 put butterfly

      $800 debit; no margin requirement.

    d. Jan 550/600/620 call butterfly

      $2,690 debit; $2,000 margin requirement.

  3. What is the Jan 550/600/620 call butterfly called? What would be your price prediction if you established this spread?

    A broken-wing or skip strike butterfly; the trader is predicting RUT will trade sideways or upward.

CHAPTER 9

Refer to the options chain in Table 9.5 for all of the following questions. This is the actual data from January 1, 2009. RUT was trading at $499.45; IV = 48.63%, and the February options had 49 days to expiration.

  1. Calculate one standard deviation. What are the closest strikes to ± 1σ?

    1σ = $89 and ±1σ = $410 to $588; closest strikes are $410 and $590.

  2. Using natural pricing (use the bid and ask), select the strikes for a Feb RUT iron condor at approximately ± 1σ. Calculate the total credit received for 15 contracts. What is the maximum possible gain in dollars for this position? What is the maximum possible loss?

    The credit for the 400/410 put spread is $0.90; the credit for the 590/600 call spread was only $0.30, so we dropped down one strike to 580/590 for a credit of $0.70. Thus, a credit of $160 per contract or $2,400 for 15 contracts. The maximum profit is $2,400 and the maximum loss is $12,600 ($15,000 – $2,400).

  3. Move the strikes of the condor above farther ITM by one strike and recalculate.

    The 410/420 put spread has a credit of $1.00 and the 570/580 call spread has a credit of $1.00 for a total of $200 per contract or $3,000 for 15 contracts. The maximum profit is $3,000 and the maximum loss is $12,000.

  4. What are the trade-offs between these two condors?

    The second condor has a higher maximum profit but a lower probability of success. The maximum loss is also reduced somewhat in the second condor. In general, the risk/reward ratio decreases as the probability of success decreases and the profitability increases.

TABLE 9.5　February Options Chain for RUT on January 1, 2009

Calls			Puts	
Bid	Ask	Strike	Bid	Ask
117.90	121.50	$380	4.80	5.70
109.60	112.30	$390	6.00	6.70
100.90	103.70	$400	7.30	7.90
92.50	95.00	$410	8.80	9.50
84.30	86.70	$420	10.50	11.20
76.30	78.70	$430	12.50	13.40
68.70	71.10	$440	14.80	15.70
61.30	63.60	$450	17.50	18.50
54.30	56.50	$460	20.40	21.50
47.80	49.70	$470	23.70	24.90
41.60	43.30	$480	27.40	28.70
35.80	37.30	$490	31.60	32.90
30.50	31.90	$500	36.20	37.60
25.70	27.00	$510	41.30	42.80
21.50	22.60	$520	46.80	48.40
17.60	18.60	$530	52.80	54.50
14.30	15.10	$540	59.20	61.10
11.40	12.20	$550	66.10	68.20
8.90	9.70	$560	73.40	75.70
6.90	7.60	$570	81.30	83.60
5.20	5.90	$580	89.00	93.00
3.80	4.50	$590	97.70	101.60
2.70	3.50	$600	106.60	110.10
1.95	2.60	$610	115.50	119.50
1.05	1.95	$620	124.90	128.80
0.55	1.40	$630	134.40	138.40

5. If you use $20 spreads for either of the above condors, what would you predict to change? Work through the calculations to confirm. Would you recommend this larger spread?

   The credit for the 390/410 put spreads is $2.10 and the credit for the 580/600 call spreads is $1.70 for a total of $380 per contract or $5,700 for 15 contracts. The maximum profit is $5,700, and the maximum loss is $24,300 ($30,000 − $5,700). The larger spread boosts the return from 19% to 23% but it more than doubles the maximum loss potential. I do not recommend wider spreads for this reason.

6. Consider the hypothetical situation with RUT trading at $500 and IV = 72%. IV has ranged from 25% to 72% over the past six months.

A 2.5-point positive skew exists between the front month and the following month.

  a. Your friend, Bubba, proposes a $500 call calendar spread that promises a 32% maximum profit.

  b. Your friend with the funny accent, Arnold, proposes an iron condor with the strikes placed at $\pm 1.5\sigma$ and a 9% maximum return.

  c. Cite the advantages and disadvantages for each trade.

> *The advantage of the calendar spread is the higher return; the disadvantage of the calendar spread is the large positive vega risk, and IV is at the top of its historical range. The advantage of the iron condor spread is its negative vega; it will gain in value as IV drops; the disadvantage of the iron condor spread is its lower return.*

  d. Which trade would you place and why?

> *The iron condor; the vega risk is too great for the calendar spread for market conditions at this time.*

7. What is the most critical piece of advice you would give someone who is considering trading the iron condor spread? Why?

> *The iron condor has a large risk/reward ratio, thus risk management techniques are crucial to avoid a large loss.*

8. What is the principal advantage of the long hedge form of condor adjustment? What is its principal disadvantage?

> *The long hedge enables you to remain in the iron condor position longer so the index may pull back and you may salvage the trade. The disadvantage of the long hedge is the requirement to invest more capital in the position.*

9. What is the principal advantage of the 200% rule form of condor adjustment? What is its principal disadvantage?

> *The 200% rule is simple and conservative. Its disadvantage is that it will close you out of many iron condor positions that could have been profitable eventually.*

10. What are the trade-offs between using the 200% rule and the long hedge forms of adjustment?

> *The returns using the 200% rule should be lower on average but have fewer swings or drawdowns. The long hedge should enable higher average returns but at the expense of taking larger losses on occasion.*

Glossary

American exercise style   Options with American style of exercise may be exercised at any time before expiration. All equity options and a small number of index options are American style in their exercise.

Ask price   The market makers post a price at which they are willing to buy the stock or option; this is the bid price. They also post a price at which they are willing to sell the stock or option; this is the ask price. The retail trader sells at the bid price and buys at the ask price. You may negotiate a better price, but think of the bid and ask as the "retail" or maximum prices at which you buy (ask price) and minimum prices at which you sell (bid price).

Assignment   The owner of an equity option contract always has the right to exercise the option by purchasing or selling shares of the underlying stock at any time before expiration. If the option that you are short is exercised, it has been assigned to you or exercised against you.

At-the-money or ATM   An option is said to be ATM when the price of the underlying stock is near the strike price of the option, e.g., if the XYZ stock price is $126.85, the XYZ $125 call and the XYZ $130 call would be considered ATM.

Automatic exercise   All options with intrinsic value of $0.01 or more are required to be exercised on the trader's behalf at expiration even though the trader did not request exercise. This process is called automatic exercise.

Bear call spread   A bearish position that is created by buying one call option and selling another call option in the same month but at a lower strike price. This is a credit spread and traders will often refer to this as "selling a call spread."

Bear put spread   A bearish position that is created by buying one put option and selling another put option in the same month but at a lower strike price. This is a debit spread, and traders will often refer to this as "buying a put spread."

Bid price   The market makers post a price at which they are willing to buy the stock or option; this is the bid price. They also post a price at which they are willing to sell the stock or option; this is the ask price. The retail trader sells at the bid price and buys at the ask price. You may negotiate a better price, but think of the bid and ask as the "retail" or maximum prices at which you buy (ask price) and minimum prices at which you sell (bid price).

Bid/ask spread   The market makers post a price at which they are willing to buy the stock or option; this is the bid price. They also post a price at which they are willing to sell the stock or option; this is the ask price. The bid/ask spread is the distance between these prices.

Black-Scholes equation   This pricing model calculates the theoretical price for an option based on the stock price, strike price, historical volatility, time to expiration, and the risk-free interest rate.

Broken-wing butterfly spread   If the distances from the sold options to the long options of the butterfly spread are not equal, a broken-wing butterfly is created. This is also known as a skip strike butterfly spread.

Bull call spread   A bullish position that is created by buying one call option and selling another call option in the same month but at a higher strike price. This is a debit spread, and traders will often refer to this as "buying a call spread."

Bull put spread   A bullish position that is created by buying one put option and selling another put option in the same month but at a higher strike price. This is a credit spread, and traders will often refer to this as "selling a put spread."

Butterfly spreads   A butterfly spread is created by selling two options and buying one option farther out-of-the-money (OTM) and one option farther in-the-money (ITM). The butterfly can be created with calls or puts.

Buy to close or BTC   An options order placed with the broker to close a short option position by buying back the short options.

Buy to open or BTO   An options order placed with the broker to open a long option position by buying options.

Calendar spread   A calendar spread is created by selling one option (a call or a put) in the current month and buying the option of the same type (a call or a put) at the same strike price in a future month. This spread is also known as a horizontal spread or a time spread.

Call option   A call option is a contract that gives the owner (the person said to be long the option) the right to buy a fixed number of shares (normally 100 shares) of the underlying stock at the strike price anytime before expiration.

Cash settlement   Equity options are always settled at exercise or expiration by the purchase or sale of the underlying stock. Index options settle in cash since no index shares exist. For example, a long call option on the Standard & Poor's 500 Index (SPX) with a strike price of $1,200 will settle with a credit of $2,300 to the trader's account if SPX closes at $1,223 at expiration.

Collar   Selling an OTM call option for a long stock position and buying a protective put option creates a collar. This limits the upside potential gains but also limits the downside potential losses.

Condor spread   A condor spread is created by using all calls or all puts to establish two vertical spreads, one above the stock or index price and one below the stock or index price. A call condor consists of a bull call spread below the current stock or index price and a bear call spread above the current stock or index price. A condor created from puts consists of a bull put spread below the current stock or index price and a bear put spread above the current stock or index price.

Contingent order A contingent order is placed with the broker with the instruction to be sent to the floor to be filled at the best available price whenever the price of a stock or index meets, exceeds, or drops below a specified trigger price.

Covered calls A covered call position is created by buying stock and selling a call option for that stock. This is also known as a *covered write* since the trader is effectively creating or writing the contract for the call option that is sold.

Credit spread When a spread is created by buying one option and selling another option, the difference in the two option prices will result in a credit (money flows into the account) if the option sold was at a higher price than the option purchased.

Debit spread When a spread is created by buying one option and selling another option, the difference in the two option prices will result in a debit (money out of the account) if the option purchased was at a higher price than the option sold.

Delta (Δ) Delta measures the change in the option price for a \$1 change in the stock price while all other variables are held constant. Delta is commonly expressed as a percentage (45%) or a decimal value (0.45) in various data sources. The delta values of calls are always positive while the delta values of puts are always negative.

Delta-neutral strategies Options trading strategies with minimal risk exposure to a change in the price of the underlying stock or index are said to be delta-neutral if the position delta is a small positive or negative value near zero.

Diagonal spread Any vertical spread may be diagonalized by buying and selling the two options in different months and at different strike prices.

Double calendar spread A double calendar spread is created by establishing a call calendar spread above the price of the underlying stock or index and establishing a put calendar spread below the price of the underlying stock or index.

Double diagonal spread One may establish two diagonal spreads, one created with calls and positioned above the current index or stock price, and one created with puts and positioned below the current index or stock price. This is the double diagonal spread, a delta-neutral options trading strategy.

Early exercise When the owner of an equity option contract chooses to exercise the option by purchasing or selling shares of the underlying stock at any time before expiration, this is known as early exercise. But this is not always possible with index options; see *European exercise style*.

European exercise style Options with European style of exercise may be exercised only at expiration. Many, but not all, index options are European style in their exercise.

Exercise   An equity option contract is exercised by purchasing or selling shares of the underlying stock at any time before expiration. Many index options may be exercised only at expiration; see *European exercise style*.

Expected return   The expected return, or risk-adjusted return, is computed by adjusting the maximum potential return for an investment by the probability of success. This is the return one may expect over time and many trades, after accounting for risk.

Extrinsic value   The difference between the value of an option if it were exercised today, its intrinsic value, and the current market price is the extrinsic value. It consists of time value and implied volatility.

Fat tails   When actual stock price data are compared with values predicted by the normal probability distribution, a larger-than-expected number of widely dispersed prices is observed, both higher and lower prices. These are the so-called fat tails of the probability distribution.

Gamma (γ)   Gamma measures the change in delta for a $1 change in the stock price while all other variables are held constant. Gamma is largest ATM and as the time to expiration nears zero.

Gaussian distribution   The normal probability distribution or "bell-shaped curve" is also known as a Gaussian distribution. The height of the curve at any given point designates the probability of occurrence for that value.

Greeks   The Greeks are quantitative measures of the sensitivity of the option's price to changes in one of several variables (such as stock price) while all other variables are held constant.

Hedge   A hedge tends to move counter to the trader's main position and thus protects that position against losses if the market moves against it. The hedge may be long stock, short stock, or a variety of options or futures positions.

Historical volatility   The value of volatility measured from the actual historical price data is the historical volatility; some authors call this the *statistical volatility*.

Horizontal spread   A horizontal spread is created by selling one option (a call or a put) in the current month and buying the option of the same type (a call or a put) at the same strike price in a future month. This spread is also known as a calendar spread or a time spread.

In-the-money or ITM   An option is said to be ITM when exercise of that option would have value; for example, if the XYZ stock price is $126.55, the XYZ $120 call is ITM and the XYZ $130 put is ITM.

Implied volatility or IV   The value of volatility entered in the Black-Scholes or other pricing model necessary to calculate the actual option price observed in the marketplace is the implied volatility. It is the volatility "implied" by the market price of the option. This is sometimes referred to as future volatility since IV is a measure of the market's consensus opinion of the future volatility for this stock price.

Intrinsic value   The value of an option if it were exercised today is the current intrinsic value.

Iron butterfly spread   The iron butterfly spread is created by selling one call option and one put option at the same strike price and buying one call option farther OTM and one put option farther OTM.

Iron condor spread   An iron condor spread is created by establishing two OTM credit spreads, one created with calls above the stock or index price and one created with puts below the stock or index price.

LEAPS   Long-Term Equity Anticipation Securities, or LEAPS, are longer-term options with expirations of as long as two years in the future.

Long   A trader is long stock or options when he has purchased the position; in the case of a long options position, the trader has a right to exercise the option and buy or sell stock.

Margin   Options trading accounts refer to margin requirements as the amount of capital held in reserve in the account until the trade is completed. This margin requirement cannot be used for any other purpose until released at the close of the position.

Married put   When the trader buys a put option to protect a long stock position, this is known as a married put.

Naked options   Whenever a trader sells an option and has no method of covering the possible exercise of that option against him with long or short stock, he is said to be "naked." A short index option is naked when a hedging position in the form of long index options is not present.

Open interest   The number of contracts for that particular option that are outstanding at that point in time is the open interest.

Options cycles   Every option has been assigned to one of three quarterly options cycles; stocks that trade options will always have options available for the current month and the following month. It will also have options available for two additional months, depending on which options cycle it falls within.

Option expiration   Monthly equity and index options expire on the Saturday following the third Friday of each month. However, broad-based index options cease trading on the Thursday before expiration.

Out-of-the-money or OTM   An option is said to be OTM when exercise of that option would have no value; for example, if the XYZ stock price is $126.55, the XYZ $130 call is OTM and the XYZ $120 put is OTM.

Put option   A put option is a contract that gives the owner (the person said to be long the option) the right to sell a fixed number of shares (normally 100 shares) of the underlying stock at the strike price anytime before expiration.

Resistance   Resistance levels are artificial price levels that tend to hold or resist the further advance of a stock price in a bullish trend. They probably occur due to a large number of traders who had decided to cut their losses if the stock returned to that price and thus are sellers at that price, slowing the advance of the stock price. A stock or index price is often said to have bounced off or broken through resistance.

Rho (ρ)   Rho measures the change in the option price for a 1% change in the risk-free interest rate. This Greek is normally only of concern for positions with LEAPS (long-term options).

Sell to Close or STC   An options order placed with the broker to close a long option position by selling the options.

Sell to Open or STO   An options order placed with the broker to open a short option position by selling the options.

Short   A trader is short stock or options when he has sold the position and has an obligation to buy the stock or options at some point in the future to close the position.

Skip strike butterfly spread   If the distances from the sold options to the long options of the butterfly spread are not equal, a skip strike butterfly is created. This is also known as a *broken-wing butterfly spread*.

Standard deviation (σ)   The standard deviation is the statistical measure of the dispersion, or width, of the probability distribution curve. Probability distributions with large standard deviations have higher probabilities of the occurrence of more extreme values.

Support   Support levels are artificial price levels that tend to hold or resist the further decline of a stock price in a bearish trend. They probably occur due to a large number of traders who had decided to add to their positions or establish a new position if the stock ever returned to that price. The entry into the market of these buyers tends to slow the decline of the stock price. A stock or index price is often said to have bounced off or broken through support.

Theta (θ)   Theta measures the change in the option price with the passage of one day to expiration while all other variables are held constant. Theta is always a negative value for an individual long option (i.e., options lose value with time).

Time decay   The value of an option decreases as time to expiration decreases, assuming all other variables are held constant. This decrease in the option's value is known as time decay. The rate of time decay accelerates as we near expiration.

Time spread   A time spread is created by selling one option (a call or a put) in the current month and buying the option of the same type (a call or a put) at the same strike price in a future month. This spread is also known as a *horizontal spread* or a *calendar spread*.

Time value   The portion of the extrinsic value of an option that is derived from the time remaining until expiration.

Vega (V) Vega measures the change in the option price for a 1% change in implied volatility while all other variables are held constant. Vega is unique among the Greeks in that it is not a Greek letter. Some financial literature uses kappa (κ) for this Greek.

Vertical spread A vertical spread is created by buying one option (a call or a put) and then selling another option of the same type (a call or a put) one or more strikes above or below the strike price of the option purchased and in the same expiration month.

VIX The VIX is the implied volatility of a theoretical option with 30 days to expiration created from the current month and the next month's ATM SPX option market prices.

Volatility skews When the volatility of two options within a spread position has different values of implied volatility, volatility skew exists. This is commonly observed in calendar spreads; when the implied volatility of the current month option is greater than the future month option, this is called a *positive volatility skew* (and vice versa for a *negative skew*).

Index